Mohammed, Jesus & Me

Amanda,

Psalm 3:3

Hazem Farraj

Hazem Farraj

ENDORSEMENTS

Hazem Farraj is an effective young minister of the Gospel of Christ. His commitment to Christ has cost him dearly, including estrangement from his family. Yet, he continues to love and serve Christ wholeheartedly, touching the lives of millions and winning people around the world to the Lord.

Paul F. Crouch,
Sr. President TBN

Hazem Farraj takes the reader on an inspiring and heartfelt journey as he receives the firsthand revelation of Christ's love. The hand of God is so clearly at work in his life as he recounts the steps that took him from a life of Islam to that of Christianity. For those who feel lost or discouraged, this story is a reminder of the unending grace of God and the plans that He has for our lives. I believe that his book will speak to people of all cultures and walks of life, presenting the power of the Lord in a real and meaningful way.

Pastor Matthew Barnett,
Co-founder of The Dream Center

I am delighted to have the opportunity to endorse the life testimony of Hazem Farraj and his book Mohammed, Jesus and Me. I have known Hazem for a number of years now, and his testimony about his experience with Jesus Christ and the transformation in his life is one of the most spiritually enriching stories you will ever hear. Having visited the Middle East over 30 times myself, and knowing the culture and sensitivity of this book, I want to encourage every reader to be very open minded to allow the Spirit of God to speak to your heart about truth. The truth of the Word of God must always be our foundation and what we live by. Mohammed, Jesus and Me is a book that will direct you to a better understanding of God's true love through His son Jesus Christ.

Perry Stone,
International Evangelist and host of Manna-Fest

Little did I know that an odd-sounding prayer would bring such a blessing into our family's life. "Salvation to Ishmael!" was not a prayer heard and proclaimed in the South! I just knew I had to pray for Ishmael's seed to come to know Jesus. Though rejection seemed to follow Ishmael, I knew that in the New Testament, Jesus loved him as much as He loved his half-brother, Isaac. Months later, we met Hazem. In Arabic, Hazem's name means "determined." I give honor to his earthly parents who named him, for "determined" he is! He has set his face toward his Savior, and through rejection, questions, disappointments and dark places, he has lived his name. This book is real and so is his faith. It is my honor to call him an adopted son.

Sandra Saylor,
Author of The Hannah Promise

Hazem Farraj is a miracle. His conversion to Christ, his walk in the Spirit, and his miracle ministry flows from a transformed life. Everyone needs to read his story. Here is a man who has become like Jesus. His love for all mankind is evident and will challenge you to love and pray for all who are religious, but lost.

Dr. Ron Phillips,
Senior Pastor Abba's House/
Central Baptist Church, Hixson TN

I still remember the first time I saw him. He came to the church where I pastor. The question was, "How did this tall, good looking kid get here?" He is Middle Eastern and talks with an accent; "not from these parts," as our locals would say. If ever I had seen the hand of the Lord lead someone, it has been so in Hazem's life. The Lord lead him, step by step, into places, and gave him favor throughout each of these steps. I don't want you to think this is some fantasy-like experience for him; He has suffered bitter disappoints, grieved for his family, and struggled for his faith. I have seen him pushed to the edge of his faith only to see him become more resolute in his commitment to Christ. You are going to thoroughly enjoy Mohammed Jesus & Me.

Harry Saylor,
Sr. Pastor Faith Fellowship Winfield AL

Hazem's story is dynamic. He ministers with compassion and his testimony is like reading a chapter in the book of Acts. His faith has stood on Christ and Christ alone, without the convenience of a church, a family, fellowships, and all the other luxuries of our American youth. His message encourages this generation to know Christ in a personal and intimate way. He has a challenging word and unique calling.

Tommy Bates,
Sr. Pastor Community Family Church

It has been my privilege to know Hazem Farraj as a fellow minister and dear friend. I believe with all my heart that God has raised Hazem up to be His crying voice in the wilderness and to prepare the way of The Lord. His ministry is absolutely crucial for God's timing to bring in the last harvest from Islam religion, and turn the hearts of the sheep that are not from this fold to find the light of the Gospel of Jesus Christ. I am so thankful that God is using His passionate message to bring hope, freedom, and deliverance to this generation! Through this book you will be able to break through the intimidation of reaching out and witnessing to others. You will be filled with God's loving heart for souls and strengthened by the power of the Holy Spirit to be a witness in Jerusalem, and in all Judea, and Samaria, and to the end of the earth!

Christine Dawood,
Author Pleasing the King

"Mohammed, Jesus & Me" made such an impression on me. All readers, whatever their religious views, will find much to stimulate their thinking in this book. The variety of life events, and the nature of these events, will provoke both thought and emotion. Hazem's story helps us see more clearly the blessings that the Lord provides when we follow Him. This book is truly an inspiration.

Elsa J. Brown,
Bondtech Corporation, President Outreach for Jesus,
Missions Director

·

Hazem Farraj was torn between family and tradition on one side, and the truth he encountered on the other side, but in a world of opportunities, he chose to lose for the sake of the truth. The hallmark of his journey was his deep love for Jesus, rather than any dislike of his tradition ... this book is worth reading many times.

Raafat Girgis, M.D.
Professor, Loma Linda School of Medicine

My meeting with Hazem was most unusual. When he walked into the Green Room at TBN and said, "Hello, I am Hazem," I reached out to shake his hand and immediately began to prophesy. The Lord showed me that God had raised him up as a strong voice to the Middle East, and he would have his own television program. (I was to learn later that a pilot program was in the making at that time). There can be no doubt this young man is called for such a time as this! He has an outstanding testimony that is a witness of the love and grace of God to all people.

Aquilla Nash,
Host of The Prophetic Whisper

I dedicate this book to all my brothers

and sisters who share my faith,

but not my freedom.

You are my heroes.

APPRECIATIONS

I am thankful for all the people who nurtured me, and saw within me, seeds of destiny, which I, myself, was unable to see.

I am forever indebted to the Bajalia Family and Steve Mashni. You came to me in Jerusalem, halfway around the world, to share the life-giving news with me. "How, then, can they call on the one they have not believed in? And how can they believe in the one of whom they have not heard? And how can they hear without someone preaching to them? And how can they preach unless they are sent? As it is written, *"How beautiful are the feet of those who bring good news!"* (Romans 10:14-15)

I am thankful for the impact that Dr. Paul Crouch and TBN have had on my life. Paul and Jan Crouch, you have been such an encouragement to me since the time I was a secret believer.

Dr. Crouch, we have dined together, we have prayed together, and we have wept together. I will never forget our Bible studies. I love you very much; as a son honors his elder father, I most gladly honor you.

Thank you to Pastor Saylor, Sandra and the whole Saylor clan. You modeled for me a beautiful picture of what a healthy family looks like, and you let me be a part of it all these years. I am certainly the man I am today because of you, Pastor Saylor. You are an inspiration and an oak tree in my life.

Thank you to Elsa Brown for her guidance when I was without direction. You sent me to school and spoke wisdom into my life. You believed in me before I believed in myself. My heartfelt appreciation and love to you and the Brown family.

For putting a microphone in my hand, pushing me up to the platform, and making me preach when I had absolutely nothing to say, I thank Mrs. Karen Wheaton. I honor you for how you pulled out of me the minister that was dormant on the inside.

Thank you to all my wonderful intercessors. The journey has been dramatic, and I'm sure your knees are sore. You have been anchors for my soul. Thank you from the bottom of my heart.

Contents

Foreword

If there was, or is, any doubt that the Bible, or the book of Acts, lives on, this book, this life, this story, this young man's journey to faith and ministry should settle it.

I still remember the first time I saw him. He came to a youth event called "Run With the Horses" at the church where I pastor. The question was, "How did this tall, good looking kid with a smile that could light up a room get here?"

He is Middle Eastern, and talks with an accent; "not from these parts," the locals would say.

For my wife Sandra and I, that's where it gets really interesting. My wife's daily habit is early morning coffee, Bible reading and prayer. During prayer, and for no particular reason, she found herself "crying out" for the seed of Ishmael, to her shock and amazement. I remember her asking if that was even legitimate, of course we knew it was. But what did it mean for us?

Now, back to Hazem. The next time we met was at the "Ramp," a powerful youth ministry, in Alabama. Something, I believe to be supernatural happened in my heart, at that time, I felt like I had to open my home to him, and give him a place to experience home.

When I got home, I talked with Sandra, and we both quickly agreed, this is what we were to do. So then we had this 17-year-old, American-born, Palestinian kid, who is a Christian, living in our home.

So, for the next two years, he lived with us and served on the ministry team "Chosen." So, again, I had to ask, how could this happen? His father, a devout Muslim, takes his family to live in Israel to immerse them into the Islamic faith, only to have his then fifteen-year-old son come to faith in Jesus Christ. Only God!

His new-found faith, unknown to his father, grew inside him to the place where, upon graduating from high school, he made the agonizing decision to leave home. If ever I had seen the hand of the Lord lead someone, it has been so in Hazem.

The Lord led him to people and places, and gave him favor. I don't want you to think this was some fantasy-like experience for him. He has suffered bitter disappointments, grieved for his family, and struggled for his faith.

Sandra and I have seen him pushed to the edge of his faith, only to see him become more resolute in his commitment to Christ.

For us, Hazem was one of those late-in-life surprises, an answer to prayer! He is a part of our family, a son in every sense. Read his story, and be challenged and blessed.

Pastor Harry Saylor

CHAPTER 1

The Neighbors

The feel of the cool limestone wall against my left palm was a welcome, if forced, distraction. I was seeking any external sensation to get my mind off the battle raging in my heart. Our home is situated on one of the sacred hills of the world's holy powder keg – Jerusalem. By historic precedent, and now by Israeli mandate, to maintain Jerusalem's reputation as the "Golden City," all the houses are made of white, reflective limestone, which, when hit by the right angle of sunlight, creates the impression of a city being showered in the glow of its glittering heavenly counterpart which will descend here on some future Day.

With my other hand, I grabbed the metal rail, and started up the stone staircase. I usually flew up the stairs but this day, I was torn. Each step seemed like a journey.

I'd take two steps and then stop to consider another facet of my dilemma.

My father, who amassed a small fortune as a grocer in one of Brooklyn's Arab enclaves, built this house in the East Jerusalem neighborhood, Beit Hanina. Our family lived on the ground floor, and we rented out the other four floors to tenants – all of whom, strangely, were Christians.

Some of our tenants were natives of the Holy Land, but the family on the second floor was American. The husband's name was Isa. Of Palestinian descent, he founded and shepherded a small church in the West Bank city Ramallah, which is about 10 miles away, but could, depending on security checkpoints, take hours to reach.

His wife's name was Alene. They both spoke with the southern drawl of their native hometown in Alabama, in the United States. She typified the incomparable hospitality of the South, which combined with Isa's Arab hospitality, made their home a warm respite for me and others like me. They also had a 9-year-old son, Jarad, who was close enough to my age of 13 to be a neighborhood playmate.

Another step....

Beit Hanina has a colorful, if bloody, history. Some scholars say the town dates back to Canaanite times. After the land's conquest by Joshua, it may have become the Benjamite suburb, Ananya, on the outskirts of the Holy City.

It's proximity to the Holy City means that Beit Hanina shared in the legacy of war and bloodshed that was visited on these parts from an immemorial time. The Babylonians, Assyrians, Greeks, Romans, Byzantines, Crusaders, Ottomans and British are just some of the invaders who have passed through and left traces of their kingdoms here.

In 1948, when Israel became a state, East Jerusalem and the rest of the West Bank, otherwise known as Judea and Samaria in the Bible, were conquered by a new landlord, the Hashemite Kingdom of Jordan. In fact, the late King Hussein of Jordan owned a multistory, light-blue railed, portico home down the block from us.

But in 1967, following the Six-Day War, Israel took over all of East Jerusalem, the West Bank, the Gaza Strip, the Golan Heights and the Sinai. Beit Hanina was brought under Israeli rule and served as something of a buffer between the Palestinian Ramallah and Jerusalem proper.

The war's end in 1967 sparked an exodus of Palestinians fleeing the instability of their war-torn homeland for the safer shores of the Western Hemisphere. When he reached manhood, my father joined that movement.

In fact, it became something like rites of passage for Palestinian men, upon reaching adulthood, to migrate to the West. There, they would work and raise enough money to marry. After a few years, they'd return to the Holy Land, find a wife, pay the dowry, celebrate with relatives and the community, and then return to their new homes in the West. After a few months, the wife would obtain legal status and join her husband in the Western Hemisphere where they would start a family.

Yaba, which means Daddy in Arabic, married my biological mother, Sabha, whom, strangely enough, was never called Yama, which means Mom or Mommy. Sabha is a native of Bettin, which is believed to be the ancient village of Bethel in the Bible. Yaba and Sabha had nine children together, six boys and three girls. The oldest is my brother Nahel who is 10 years my senior. I am the youngest. Perhaps that is why I don't really know why we never addressed her as Mom. I must have just followed suit, hearing my siblings, all of whom were older, calling her Sabha. The funny thing is that I don't even remember thinking it was weird that we called her by her first name. I mean, we called our father Yaba, so wouldn't it have made sense that we called our mother Yama?

In terms of hard knocks, having to raise all of us would have probably been enough for my mother to lose her peace of mind at the very least, but add that to her struggling with the emotions and feelings of being an unhappy wife, whether or not my father intended to cause her any pain, and the formula for a woman in despair was born. At the time, I was too young to know, or understand, my parents' issues, and even as an adult, all I can do is reflect on the memories I do have.

One day, when I was five years old, I came home from kindergarten to find my mother packing her bags. Yaba was at work and wouldn't be home for hours. My brothers and sisters were all unusually quiet. Standing in the living room, which faced the bedroom, I remember watching them all look back and forth at each other, and then at Mom. No one was talking or asking questions. It was like they knew something. Their looks worried me, but what could possibly be wrong? Mom moved hurriedly, occasionally mumbling a few words to herself, flashing a smile at no one in particular. If felt like those smiles were meant for us.

She finished packing and zipped up her luggage.

Why is she moving so fast? I wanted to know, but couldn't even imagine a list of possible answer choices. I was baffled.

With her packed bags in hand, she looked at us, and flashed another smile that could have meant a million different things. She said she was going to visit her sick mother and would be back. Breathing heavily, lugging her bags, she scurried out the door and closed it behind her.

When she walked out, I ran over to one of the two windows overlooking the street, and I pushed my face up against the glass to watch her. Something didn't feel right at all.

After a few seconds, I felt a pang of emptiness. Maybe it was a culmination of all the impressions I had gotten that afternoon; the looks on everyone's faces; Mom's strange and hurried departure; and slowly, the traumatizing realization that she wasn't coming back.

I felt as if someone had thumped on my chest. The pain of the thump was quickly followed by this dark, tangible hollowness against which I could hear echoes of my heart beating. Knowing something, but not sure what, I pressed my face against the glass and cried. She was gone. That was all I knew.

Yaba his tried best to fill the void in our home. There was no time to think about what happened or why. I guess my siblings and I all had a pretty good idea about what went down, but we must have concluded that it was better to keep quiet about it all. At first, my father tried to be both Mom and Dad to all of us. If he was hurting, it didn't show.

One day, my dad even attempted to prepare my favorite meal, maklooba, a popular Palestinian meal of rice, potatoes and chicken. Considering his limited English language skills, my father had attained stunning success as a businessman in the US, but watching him in a kitchen, this was another story altogether.

Earnestly and swiftly, he moved back and forth between the stove, the sink, and the refrigerator. The pots and pans were stacked high. The occasional cuss word, as he dropped a glass, or touched a hot pan handle, was enough to elicit a giggle from us.

At dinnertime, we all gathered in the dining room. Our emotions were still raw and visible on our faces. We didn't need to express pain verbally because what had broken was broken inside all of us at the same time, and it was nothing any of us could fix. It wasn't just that Mom wasn't there. It was as if a central piece of each one of us had disappeared, and we knew there was no need, for the time being, to look for that missing piece.

No one seemed to care what the food tasted like; that the potatoes were raw; that the chicken was slimy, or that the rice was hard and crunchy. We sat together in an understood silence. When so much happens to you so fast, without your permission, you learn to brace yourself for whatever might come next. No one finished their dinner that night, and Yaba didn't make a big deal about it.

After a few months of trying to be both parents to us, Yaba married my stepmother, Ribhia. She was nice to us when we were young. A Palestinian woman, she did her best to be a good mother, but the nine of us were an awesome responsibility to take on.

In time, she would give birth to four of her own beautiful children. These are my sisters and brothers regardless if we have different mothers or not. It is not customary in my culture to use terms like "half" sister or "half" brother. In fact, adding the "half," in my opinion, maybe because of my upbringing, seems to devalue a sibling relationship, and I love ALL of my siblings way too much to do that. While I immediately felt love for her offspring, my siblings, I also immediately understood the reality that I was not her "real" son. By this, I simply mean that I saw a different kind of love shared between her and her biological children. It was pure, and it seemed to require no effort at all. With us, all nine of us, it must have been overwhelming for her to act in place of our mother. She tried her best, but we were already so destroyed on the inside that it didn't matter what she did or didn't do. We were broken and she seemed to be going through the motions. When her biological children were born, being a mom seemed easier for her. Seeing that mother-child bond brought back that same black pang I felt that day at the window when my mom left for some reason. By this time, I was adept at pushing it down. I learned something else too -- one of the clearest indicators of our value is the degree to which our pain is allowed to be expressed. This belief seared itself into my consciousness.

Step...

To protect us from the "corrupting" influences of American culture, Yaba eventually brought us back to his homeland. I was 12 years old when we moved to Beit Hanina.

I was enrolled in Bridge Academy; an English language school which was tailored to help students, like me, improve our knowledge of the Arabic language and Islamic religion. I already could speak Arabic, and I knew about Islam, but in Jerusalem, I was also completely immersed in the ethnic and spiritual culture of my people.

Step, step…

Although it was all-encompassing and affected every aspect of our lives, the political tension in the Holy Land was not my primary concern. I was more interested in religion. I felt a spiritual void in my heart that often propelled me to greater observance of the pillars of Islam: prayer, alms, fasting, recitation of the creed and pilgrimage to Mecca.

Feelings of guilt haunted me as I found myself unable to wholeheartedly live the strict Islamic lifestyle I was taught. I always assured myself that if I only obeyed the precepts of Islam more thoroughly, I would discover true spiritual happiness. To assuage those feelings of guilt, I would often go on week-long periods of strict observance. I would read the Koran and pray at least four times a day. The Faj'r, or early morning prayers, were way too early for me, but I would make them up with extra prayers at noontime. I would also abstain from any activities that I considered sinful.

The excitement of feeling right with "Allah" provided the impetus that kept me going for weeks. But at the end of each of those periods, I'd find that I was still the same. There was no change inside. Nothing was different. The emptiness was still there. Those feelings of disappointment invariably turned into hopelessness, and the hopelessness into apathy.

A few more months would pass, and I'd find the inner drive to go at it again, but I'd invariably end up in the same predicament. It became a frustrating and futile cycle in my life.

The American family on the second floor provided me with a sense of challenge I hadn't felt before. I knew they were Christians, and I knew what the Koran said about Christians and Christianity. In the days of the Prophet Mohammed, Christians were forced to convert, pay the "jizya" penalty for not accepting Islam, or die. Of course, I had no intention of hurting them.

What concerned me was the far more dreadful fate that awaited them on Judgment Day when they would walk across a sword (Sirat Al Mostaqeem) that was suspended over hell. For not accepting Islam, they would fall into the flames where they would be tormented for all eternity.

I really liked Isa, Alene and Jarad and was afraid for their souls, so much so, that I took it on as a personal challenge to win these Christians to Islam. If I won this battle, it would also strengthen my commitment to Islam and disprove my lingering fears and doubts.

At first, I brought my Koran upstairs to show them verses about the corruption of Christianity. I also showed them how the Koran insists that Jesus is not the Son of God. A whole sura, or chapter in the Koran, is devoted to denying the divine son-ship of Jesus.

There was another intriguing element about the missionary couple upstairs. The husband, Isa, was legally blind. His vision was 200 over 200. Although he functioned independently without a cane or a guide, he could barely discern the light and shadows around him. When he would speak to you, he'd turn his head slightly to the left. It looked like he was talking past you, but you knew you had his undivided attention.

His limited vision seemed to accentuate his depth of spiritual vision. It felt sometimes like he could see right through a situation and deal with the crux of an issue that those of us with 20/20 vision missed.

Having lived in Ramallah for the best of 15 years, he was well known, and well loved, even by those who disagreed with his theologies. His handicap, in a sense, endeared him to others, even those who were otherwise put off by his Christianity.

His fierce unwillingness to be dependent on others seemed to be confirmed by his huge muscles. He was a weight lifting fanatic who regularly worked out at the neighborhood gym and kept himself in tip top shape. All these factors combined to form the man who God used to help open my eyes to the truth. It was almost poetic how his physical limitation seemed to mirror my spiritual condition.

I must admit, I felt a little conflicted to bring up the subject of his vision, but it was common knowledge among Christians and Muslims that Jesus healed the eyes of the blind.

"You say Jesus is alive, right?" I asked Isa and Alene.

"Yes, He is alive," they answered in unison.

"Then why hasn't he healed your eyes?" I asked, thinking my question would shake them and cause them to doubt their God, but it didn't.

So I asked another question, "How could you walk around Jerusalem like you do when you're legally blind?"

"It's by the grace of God," Isa said.

I was flummoxed. "Grace of God"? What does that mean? How does it apply to his situation? Sure, I had heard the Arabic words "Na'emit Allah" before, which means "grace of God," but I had never heard it used in such a relevant, powerful and personal way.

They listened to me patiently and politely. They seemed genuinely concerned for me. Then, the wife, Alene, finally said to me, "We listened to you, now will you listen to us?"

"Of course," I replied.

They proceeded to talk about Jesus Christ. What amazed me was that they spoke about Him as if they knew Him personally. Their faith wasn't just based on philosophy or ideas, but an actual relationship with God. They talked about miracles He had done in their lives. I listened to them, but I knew I was right. I had to win this battle. I had to bring them to Islam.

I started coming up to their home and challenging them with even harder questions, "How could Jesus be God and the Son of God? Who was controlling the universe when Jesus was on earth if He is God? How could God die on a cross? How could God be hungry? How could God allow His Son to die such a painful and shameful death when He had the power to rescue Him?"

What amazed me weren't just their answers, but the boldness and conviction in their responses. They were never shaken at my incessant needling and prodding. They didn't yell at me. They didn't respond in anger, or hatred, or defensiveness. Instead, they would gently answer all my questions with stunning clarity, logic and persuasiveness.

They persisted in their unflinching love towards me. I was dumbfounded. Why were they so nice? Why did they care about me? I really started feeling like I was part of their family. It was a wonderful feeling I never felt before. I so longed to be loved in this way.

Not long after I started challenging them, Isa and Alene told me they wanted me to meet one of their friends, Steve.

I had already met him several times before but they told me that he had a unique understanding of my situation, but I wasn't sure what that "unique understanding" was. I knew Steve as an American who had come to work with Isa's church. He played guitar and sang. He spoke broken Arabic with a back hills dialect. We often laughed at his accent.

He often engaged in our discussions about religion, but I never noticed anything particularly outstanding about his contribution to our discussions until one day. It was during the month of Ramadan, and I was fasting. The most important day of Ramadan is day 27, which is called "Lailat al Qadar," or "Night of Power." Some call it the "Night of Wishes."

It is believed to be the night that Mohammed started receiving the Koran from the Angel Gabriel. It is also believed that a prayer offered on that night is worth 10,000 prayers offered on any other night. Those 10,000 prayers would be added to a Muslim's good works when his deeds are weighed on a scale on Judgment Day. Many Muslims spend the whole night in prayer at their local mosques on this night.

One of the folk beliefs that have come to be associated with the Night of Power is that a Muslim could ask for anything he wants on that night at precisely the moment that the "power" is manifested (some say around 2 a.m. or 3 a.m.), and it will be granted. I had heard these stories before.

As we talked about Lailat al Qadar, Steve said that when he was a child living in the West Bank village of Deir Dibwan, he used to try to stay up for the Night of Power so he could ask for 100 tacos. Having been raised in the U.S., he loved Mexican food, but there were no Mexican restaurants in his village.

We all laughed at the childish request but his words intrigued me. Why would a Christian be making a request on the Night of Power? Why would a Christian even know about, or believe in, Lailat al Qadar?

Step. Step.

The love I felt at Isa and Alene's house filled a void in my heart. Before long, I wasn't trying to win them to Islam anymore. I was just so overcome with their love and care. I didn't feel that kind of love and acceptance in my own family. The more I fought it, the more I felt drawn to be with them.

I had always felt a sense of alienation, and being in Jerusalem only added to that feeling.

Am I American? Am I Arab? Am I a hybrid? Where do I belong? Who am I?

As a teenager, I struggled with all these questions. I didn't really feel like I belonged anywhere. And even though I was Arab and Muslim, I felt different, even from my own siblings.

But I didn't feel that alienation around Isa and Alene. They never made me feel like I was an inconvenience to them. They never seemed too busy for me. Their door was always open to me, and more importantly, I could tell, their hearts were always open. Their love was unconditional. It didn't matter if I was Arab, American or whatever. It didn't even matter if I was a Muslim or a Christian. Their love was the same.

They often had guests from America who would visit them, and they always introduced me as if I was part of their family.

After months of visiting their home, I decided to take a bold step and visit their church. Of course, my family didn't know about this.

Isa and Alene worked for a Christian school in the West Bank, called Jerusalem School. I met some of the other teachers and workers from the school. Most of them were Americans, and I really enjoyed being with them. I felt the same love and acceptance I felt with Isa and Alene from these people. They seemed to embrace me and care for me even though they knew I was a Muslim.

The Saturday night meeting was held in the Nazarene Church in

Jerusalem, about 500 yards from the Old City. The two-story church was a fixture in this Jerusalem neighborhood. I had passed by it many times, but this is the first time I actually came inside. In fact, it was the first time I ever entered any church.

I walked through the large, black, metal gate onto the chipped-stone driveway. As I ascended the stairs, I had second thoughts.

Should I be here? What's going to happen to me?

I assuaged these fears by remembering that I was with Isa, Alene, Jarad and the other teachers who were so friendly to me.

Passing through the foyer, I saw the huge room with cathedral ceilings and stained glass windows on either side. There were rows of long cushioned, mahogany benches. They looked long enough to seat 10 people each. There was an aisle through the middle of the rows leading up to the pulpit, with a prominent gold cross on the facade, and a chrome microphone stand on top.

I scanned the room for doors in case I needed to escape. To the left of the pulpit, I saw a small door leading downstairs. In spite of my own fears, I felt no pressure from anyone. I sat in the back. I didn't want to be too close to the pulpit or to the other people. They were all dear friends, but we were different from each other.

I am a Muslim, and they are Christians, and they know it, I thought.

I felt alone.

It eased my anxieties a little that the worship leader standing behind the pulpit and strumming his guitar was Steve. He was singing songs about Jesus. The people were all lifting their hands and clapping. It was so comforting, but the peace I felt inside scared me. I was afraid that if I got any closer, I might be infected with their joy. It wasn't what I expected at all. The peace and love I felt was so different from my experiences in the mosque.

After a few minutes, I got up and scuttled my way down the narrow side aisle, through the small door, and down the stairs to the basement. I found a quiet room where I stretched out my imaginary rug, and prayed to Allah, the god of Islam, I had so sought to please.

My prayer was recitation. It was the same words I prayed so many times before. I was hoping that by going through this ritual, the inner turmoil would subside. I would be convinced once and for all, and I would be steadfast in the religion I inherited from my family. All my doubts would go away.

After prayer, I went back upstairs. The music was over and the sermon had begun. I listened politely, but my heart was squirming to the left and right, trying to avoid the penetrating light of truth I felt emanating from that pulpit. I smiled courteously, but turmoil was raging inside my heart.

Then Steve got up to sing a song he said he had written about me. He used to jokingly refer to me as HazMat (short for hazardous material). This song was based on that nickname:

"A hazardous material is about to be unleashed/

Against the kingdom of the devil/ It's about to be released/

And though the dark of night may seem/ to linger for so long/

The strength of the Risen One/ Will always make you strong/

Hands...He has him in His hands/ has him in His hands/

Hazem in his hands forever/

And though there might be battles/ and though the devil fights/

He can never win/ Because of Him who brings you light/

You're in His hands/

Has him in His hands/ Hazem in his hands/

Hazem in His hands forever."

Step....

That was last night. I'm walking up these stairs, now, to take an even bigger step. I think. I know enough about Islam to know what this step will mean for me, mean for my family. The same way I felt alone in the church for those few moments last night, I now felt alone in my own home. Something was different inside of me now. I needed to know what was happening.

CHAPTER 2

The Key of David

I walked up the last stair, took two steps to the right, and stood in front of Isa's door. Like most doors in Jerusalem, it was metal with a small, rectangular-shaped, beveled glass window that was surrounded by decorative metal swirls. I had seen this sort of thing hundreds of times and never paid much attention, but for this moment, I just felt like standing there and staring at the designs.

If I knocked, the door would be opened. If it opened, I would go in. If I went in, they would ask me about last night, and I would tell them. A torrent of thoughts rushed through my mind. If I cross this threshold, there would be no turning back.

My right hand went up, and with a sense of passion, I knocked. Isa answered. As usual, he was talking on his red Nokia cell phone. The Arabs call them "Jawals" after the name of the largest Palestinian cell phone company.

Without talking to me, Isa pointed to the living room. I went in and sat on the sofa against the back wall. He walked over to the kitchen so he could hear better. The TV was on. I sat and watched, hoping against hope, that he would be too busy to talk to me. But in a few minutes, Isa came out of the kitchen. He was his normal self; cheerful, kind and inquisitive. And, of course....

"What did you think of the meeting last night?"

I expected the question, but I didn't plan how I would answer. I looked up at Isa standing in front of me, and quickly looked down, focusing on the design of the floor tiles. This lasted for several awkward minutes.

Then, in an unexpected burst of motivation, I got up and pulled a wooden chair from the dining room table. I put it right in front of the couch where Isa was now sitting.

"Something is happening inside me, I want to become a Chr, Chr..." I said. To my shock, the word "Christian" wouldn't come out.

"I want to become a Chrrr..."

Finally, after about a half hour of me wrestling with the words, Isa said that he had to leave to go to an appointment. With all the strength I had in me, I stood up. I said, "I want to become a Christian."

I might have said it differently now, but at the time, all I knew was that I was making the dangerous decision to change my religion. I was so scared, but so sure at the same time. I tried to put out of my mind what my father would do if he knew.

Steve was outside on the patio playing his guitar. Isa called him in. He told Steve what I said. He then told me that Steve, like me, had been a Muslim. I looked at Steve and, somehow, it felt like I already knew that. Then, I realized this is why Steve had knowledge about believing in Laylat Al Qadr. He was once a Muslim too!

Isa asked Steve to pray with me.

As if he knew what I was thinking, Steve said, "You're not just changing your religion. You're changing families. You're coming to the family of God to be his son."

I looked at him; I was speechless and trembling inside.

"Repeat after me," he said. "God, I am a sinner..."

"God I am a sinner...."

"Forgive me for my sins..."

"Forgive me for my sins..."

"Come into my heart, and give me a new life. I believe, Jesus, that You died for me, and came back to life in three days. Thank You, Jesus, for dying for me. I want to follow You, every day, for the rest of my life. Amen."

The inner turmoil was instantly replaced by the tangible sense of God's presence that I had been searching for, for so long. I remember thinking during that prayer how something inside of me was revived. I was awakened. Had I known what shouting and praising God in the Christian faith looked like, I would have responded to what I was feeling by doing that. In fact, it was all I could do to hold myself down and act dignified. I didn't want these two men to think I was crazy, but there, on the inside of me, was a party, and I had never felt that before. I literally felt like a huge burden was lifted off my shoulders. I threw my head back and laughed. I was experiencing joy unspeakable and full of glory.

We all hugged and rejoiced together. I couldn't stop smiling. The joy was so real. For so long, I longed to experience God's tangible presence, and here it was.

Pastor Isa told me that I had to learn to pray to God every day. But it wasn't the rote prayer that I had learned as a Muslim. It was a living conversation with my Heavenly Father. I was to speak to Him, and share all my cares. It was exactly what I had wanted for so long.

Pastor Isa also gave me a small copy of the New Testament. It was a lime-green Gideon Bible with a golden lamp-of-knowledge imprint on the cover. He told me to read it every day.

This was the threshold I was afraid to cross, but now I crossed it, and I knew that it was the right decision. Like Jesus said, "Anyone who chooses to do the will of God will find out whether my teaching comes from God." When I chose to do His will, I discovered that He truly is God. The joy in my heart was from heaven. In Islam, I never found joy or peace.

I kept going up to Isa's house on a daily basis to learn more about the Bible. Many times, Isa and Alene weren't home, and I'd find Steve there. He started teaching me some guitar chords and some Christian Arabic songs.

One day I was struggling in my newfound faith. I felt so alone in my home with my Muslim family.

What if my faith failed? What if I wasn't able to continue on this path? What would happen to me? Would God send me to hell?

I went upstairs and Steve was there. I came to find out that Steve's real name was Husein. He was born and raised in the U.S. but had lived in his father's village, Deir Debwan, as a child. Having been a Muslim, he came to the Lord through a visitation of the Holy Spirit when he was 15 years old. His story was so much like my own.

What also intrigued me was the reason he was in Isa's home. He had been threatened for preaching the Gospel in Ramallah. Some militants found out that he had been a Muslim and was now preaching to Muslims. They threatened to kill him if he didn't leave Ramallah. Since he had been working with him in Ramallah, he came and stayed with Pastor Isa until he could find his own place.

I told Steve about my feelings and my fears for the future. We talked a while in the living room and then moved into the kitchen. I told him how I was concerned that I would fail as a Christian, and how I was afraid that if my family found out about me, they might force me to go back to Islam.

Steve reiterated to me what he said when I accepted the Lord. I had not changed my religion. It wasn't that I was a Muslim who became a Christian. Rather, I had become a son of God, through the power of the Holy Spirit, and by the blood of Jesus.

As we stood in the kitchen, he told me how much God loved me, and how much He cared for me. Then a fantastic thing happened. Steve quoted what he said was one of his favorite scriptures: "Not one sparrow falls without Your heavenly Father knowing, of how much more value are you…."

Instantly, a bird fell on the kitchen windowsill and sat between us. It was a powerful confirmation of the words. We were so overjoyed at God's faithfulness to confirm His word. That was one of the first miracles I experienced in Jerusalem.

Aware that I had to be careful about expressing my Christianity in front of my family, Steve also encouraged me to watch Christian television programs that were broadcasting in Jerusalem. He told me about TBN which was on 24 hours a day. One day, I watched a film about Jesus' life. I was gripped by it, and I was so overjoyed at the end when they showed the way of salvation. Although I knew that I was already saved, I prayed the sinner's prayer with them again.

My faith seemed to grow day by day. Every night before going to sleep,

I used to read the lime-green New Testament Isa had given me. I hid it under the Persian carpet next to my bed. In the dark, with a flashlight, I would read it when no one else was around. When I was done, I would return it to its place under the carpet.

One afternoon, while I was at school, I had a strange feeling come over me. I heard that voice inside loudly say, "Give back that Bible." I somehow knew that someone had found the Bible. When I got home, my intuition proved right. My 5-year-old sister greeted me at the door and said, "You're in trouble." She said it in a mocking way. I could tell that she herself didn't understand what was going on.

My stepmother had been cleaning my room when she pulled back the carpet and found the little green book. It still baffles me to this day how my stepmother knew where to look to find it. A formidable woman, my stepmother knew she had tremendous power over me in that she could tell my father what she had found.

That day was hellacious for me. I turned the house upside down looking for the book. For hours, I looked and looked and finally, I found it. It was under my stepmother's pillow. This meant that she would be asking me about it eventually. I wondered frantically what I should say. I could not think of a good excuse.

Why did I have a New Testament, and why were there songs written about Jesus in there, in my own handwriting?

Around 8:30 pm, she called me to her room. She walked towards the pillow and grabbed the New Testament. Holding the book in her right hand, she waved it back and forth. The ominous look in her eye, along with her tone of voice, sent a chill down my spine.

"What is this?"

This was it, the defining moment. I would have to tell her everything. As I opened my mouth to begin speaking, I heard words shoot out of my mouth; words that were unplanned. I literally heard them coming out of my mouth, and was stunned by them.

"I am studying world religions in my school." I actually was studying world religions, so that wasn't a lie.

That answer satisfied her and she just said, "OK. Give this back to your teacher and tell him you don't want to learn Christianity."

And it was over. I walked away unscathed, unharmed and even stunned.

Later, I read Mark 13:11: "… don't worry in advance about what to say. Just say what God tells you at that time, for it is not you who will be speaking, but the Holy Spirit." I felt that the scripture had been fulfilled that afternoon in my life.

It didn't take long to realize that I was living in the heart of the Bible land. Our hometown was on the very outskirts of the city where Jesus had preached, performed many miracles, died and rose again. It was the land where the prophets lived, ministered and died.

I always knew this land was special, and it was called the Holy Land, but I was also perplexed by the contradiction I was seeing before me. While it was called "holy" and "blessed," it was such a land of conflict and bloodshed.

Shortly after my conversion, in October 2000, the whole land seemed to break out into spontaneous force. Seemingly, out of nowhere, violence exploded across the whole country.

Following the failure of American-mediated peace talks between Bill Clinton, then Palestinian President Yasser Arafat and, then Israeli Prime

Minister Ehud Barak, the situation in the land became tense.

It was also nearing the time for Israeli elections, and one of the candidates for Prime Minister, Ariel Sharon, walked on the Dome of the Rock/Al Aqsa compound with an enormous security entourage in an effort to show that Jews had the right to visit the site, which was conquered by Israel in the 1967 war.

There are two mosques on the Al Aqsa compound: The Dome of the Rock and the Al Aqsa mosque. Together they form Islam's third holiest site, after the cities of Mecca and Medina, which are in Saudi Arabia.

Muslims believe that Abraham almost offered his son, Ishmael, to God on the rock around which the Dome of the Rock was built. It is also believed that Mohammed was brought to this site from Saudi Arabia on the back of Al Burraq, a winged horse that was guided by the angel Gabriel. From the stone, Muslims believe Mohammed was taken to the seven heavens where he met the prophets, including Moses and Jesus.

But while to Muslims the Al Aqsa Compound is the third holiest site, to Jews, it is the holiest of all sites. The same yellowing limestone platform is, to the Jews, the Temple Mount where they believe the temples of Solomon and Herod stood. All that remains of those ancient Jewish structures is the Western Wall, which is part of the stone foundation where the temples stood. It is called the Kotel, and the Wailing Wall, where written prayers are inserted into the cracks between the stones.

This compound has rightly been called the most contentious piece of real estate in the world. The stone at the heart of the conflict is inside the Dome of the Rock. The Jews call it "The Foundation Stone." Like their Arab cousins, they also believe it is the site where Abraham almost offered his son, Isaac, on Mount Moriah. It is also believed to be the threshing floor of Araunah the Jebusite, where King David saw the angel with his sword outstretched over Jerusalem. Fearing God's judgment, David purchased the threshing floor and built an altar to God upon it. Solomon would later build the First Temple atop the sacred stone. Some even believe the stone is the exact location of the Holy of Holies, upon which the Ark of the Covenant rested in Solomon's Temple.

The site took on a new significance in 1967 after Israel conquered East Jerusalem with the Old City. A new, Messianic fervor arose as many saw the return of Jerusalem to Jewish control as being one of the signs of the Second Coming of Jesus.

One of the prerequisites to His return, many believe, is that a third temple will be built in Jerusalem. Most of the implements for this new temple, including a large solid gold menorah, have already been made, and are stored in the Temple Institute near the Temple Mount.

Many in the Muslim world are aware of these beliefs and fear that the Dome of the Rock and Al Aqsa mosques would have to be destroyed to make room for the new temple.

Following the 1967 conquest of Jerusalem, Israeli General Moshe Dayan walked into the Dome of the Rock mosque to assure its Muslim landlords that Israel would not endanger the mosques or infringe on the Muslims religious practices. Furthermore, Israel agreed to let the Islamic Waqf oversee the administration of the two mosques and the surrounding compound.

As to what actually started the violent uprising, there are two narratives. In the Palestinian narrative, Ariel Sharon's visit to the Temple Mount, with the 1,000 member security force, sparked the uprising in October 2000. But from the Israeli point of view, the uprising was commissioned by Yasser Arafat immediately upon the failure of the Camp David talks between himself, Bill Clinton and Ehud Barak.

Whatever the actual spark, it grew into a furious blaze that threatened to consume the entire Middle East. Palestinian young men rose in what would come to be known as the "Al Aqsa Intifada" or uprising.

Arab and Muslim countries linked arms with the Palestinians in their resistance against Israel. The Arab world was inflamed by the non-stop live coverage of Palestinians being wounded and hauled out on stretchers as they fought with stones against the Israeli forces.

A theme of those early days of the Intifada was a David and Goliath scenario. Israel with the most powerful military in the Middle East, and the fifth most powerful military in the world, was shown to be fighting boys with stones in the streets. It was clearly an unbalanced fight, but an effective media campaign quickly incited the Palestinian masses.

Thousands of Palestinians took to the streets in protest, and the killing began on both sides.

I was in the 10th grade at this time. It was so painful to see the people being killed every day. At times, I even got angry. I had heard how Jesus was a Jew, but what I saw around me from the Jewish people, was that they were fighting my people, the Palestinians.

The conflict dominated our lives in every possible way. Some schools became recruitment centers for aspiring nationalists, and the mosques proclaimed, incessantly, the virtues of Jihad (holy war) and the Shahids (martyrs) of the intifada, whose numbers swelled day by day.

Even popular music was inundated with messages of Jihad and the Palestinian struggle. A common theme in many songs was the return of Jerusalem to Islamic control. One of the most famous Arab singers sang these words, "The last word with us is Jerusalem is our land. The truth is the truth and the right is our right."

Another popular song described a Palestinian boy being killed on his way to school, carrying his brand new book bag. Against the backdrop of these heart-wrenching vignettes, a choir chants, hauntingly, "Jerusalem will return to us Jerusalem will return to us."

Having grown up in the West, I was unaccustomed to the culture of violence that I was seeing around me. Daily, there was news of suicide bombers and bus bombings. Hundreds of Israelis were brutally killed in the suicide and bus bombing campaign that was unleashed.

Israeli retaliation was swift and severe. Thousands of Palestinians were killed and maimed in the conflict, which raged from 2000-2005.

I never participated in any of the demonstrations, but the mere fact of my being here and being Palestinian made me, by default, a member of one of the parties to this conflict. I was working a summer job at an Arabic confection shop when Israeli soldiers stormed in seeking some stone throwers. As I was cleaning tables, one of them grabbed me from behind and slammed me against a wall. His index finger was on the trigger of his M16 rifle, and he was taking his vengeance out on me. Although he beat me up, I was just glad that he didn't pull the trigger. At one point, he threw me over the tables and grabbed my throat and squeezed hard enough to leave his finger imprints.

When it was over, I thought to myself, "Thank you Jesus."

When the first soldier finished, round two began with a different soldier. I said in English that I was an American citizen so he'd leave me alone. He did.

When I got home that night, my father saw the bruises on my neck and asked me what happened. I told him about what the soldiers did to which he responded, "Welcome to the Palestinian plight."

Its location on the northern rim of Jerusalem made my neighborhood one of the hottest spots of the early days of the Intifada. Checkpoints were erected right in front of my home. We heard the crackling sounds of gunfire, the static of army speakers, and the blaring of car horns, as drivers were forced to wait for hours at the checkpoint.

From our roof, we'd sometimes watch the red streams of helicopter-launched missiles that disappeared into neighboring communities. The cacophony was inevitably followed by the wail of ambulance sirens, picking up more of the wounded, and transporting them to badly overcrowded hospitals.

To escape the violence, my father decided to bring us all back to the U.S. We packed our things and got ready to vacate our floor level home. I was torn inside. While I loved Jerusalem, I understood my father's concern.

But there was something else that was bothering me.

A few days before leaving Jerusalem, I knelt down beside my bed, crying with a hurting heart. I asked my Messiah who I had met only nine months earlier, "If your people are the Jews, why are they killing my people, the Palestinians?"

I admit, it felt like a biased prayer, but nonetheless, it was my prayer, and it expressed the frustration I was feeling inside. What's amazing is what followed.

Immediately, I fell into a deep sleep. The next thing I knew I was in an unknown place, and into the darkness walked a man. His face was very priestly, and his wardrobe was a mix between a shepherd and a priest. His hair was dark brown and seemed long enough to be upon his shoulders. It was not straight. He had a long face and a very dark, not too thick, beard.

He walked up, stood in front of me, and uttered the words, "Read Isaiah 22." That was all he said. He turned around and walked back into the darkness. I knew upon waking up, I had encountered a high priest of sorts, even though I had no idea what the words high priest even meant.

Who was Isaiah? And what did Isaiah 22 even mean? I felt like I encountered Jesus, but I didn't want to sound like a nut.

When I shared the vision with Isa and Alene, they asked me, "Hazem, do you know we have a prophet named Isaiah?"

I had no clue! And little did I know, there was an Isaiah 22 in the Bible. In fact, I didn't even own a complete Bible. I was so amazed that I had heard from Jesus!

I was even more astonished when I actually read what it said in the first verses of Isaiah 22. "What is happening? Why is everyone running to the rooftops? The whole city is in a terrible uproar. What do I see in this reveling city? Bodies are lying everywhere..."

It felt as if I was reading a newspaper, not a 3,000 year old prophecy. The words described exactly what was happening around us. People were gathering daily on their housetops, watching the fighting, listening to the raids and helicopters, and watching the missiles being launched.

The Israeli newspapers and the Arab television stations were filled with the pictures of the victims of the suicide bus bombings, and images of the Palestinians victims on the other side. But it was the next verses that gripped my heart, "That's why I said, 'Leave me alone to weep; do not try to comfort me. Let me cry for my people as I watch them being destroyed."

Here was the God of the universe expressing the same emotions that I was feeling. He used almost the same words I had used in my prayer. Never in Islam did I have a feeling that God was weeping for the people. But here, God was like a brokenhearted father, watching his children, and weeping, refusing comfort because of the greatness of His pain.

But what really grabbed my attention were the cryptic words of verse 22, "I will give him the key to the house of David—the highest position in the royal court. When he opens doors, no one will be able to close them; when he closes doors, no one will be able to open them."

The key of David? Who was this who would have the Key of David? I asked my missionary friends and they told me to read these verses in Revelation 3 in the New Testament, "This is the message from the one who is holy and true, the one who has the key of David. What he opens, no one can close; and what he closes, no one can open."

The verse is about Jesus! He was the One whose heart is broken. As I looked around me, I saw that both the Jews and the Muslims had refused the salvation of the Messiah Who came and died for them and rose again. He is the One who holds the key. The Key is Jesus. Without Him, there is no inner peace, and there is no political or national peace.

The gist of what I believe the Lord Jesus showed me through Isaiah 22 is that, He, too, was heartbroken for his people and mine. They were killing each other over land and politics, and both were missing the point! I was also impressed by verse 4, where God says, "…depart from; let me to weep bitterly for my people. Do not try to comfort me."

The God of Heaven suddenly was weeping along with me, a nobody kid in Beit Hanina, Jerusalem.

CHAPTER 3

Imaginary Cuffs

With the political situation in the Holy Land deteriorating day by day, my father brought us back to the U.S. Instead of the bustling streets of Brooklyn where I was born and raised, we moved to the "Sunshine State," Florida, where my father opened a convenience store.

At 15 years old, I was now a sophomore at Miami Springs Senior High School. I found it easy to get back in the groove of being a student in an American school. I was also a Christian now which I thought might make it easier to fit in with the Americans. After all, I was one of them now!

To many Middle Easterners, America is considered a Christian country in the same way that Saudi Arabia is considered a Muslim country to many Americans. Having lived here before, I knew that wasn't the case, but I did think that I would have greater freedom to live my Christianity here.

Instead, I received a painful crash course in Western Christianity. At my father's store, I often saw a man we called "The Preacher." He was one of our most frequent customers; always buying liquor. The worst part is that he used church funds to buy the excessive amounts of liquor he'd consume. He would also buy hundreds of lottery tickets and instant scratch-off cards. Through him, my family was getting a warped picture of Jesus, and this angered me.

Here I was, a secret believer who felt my decision to follow Christ could end up costing me my life, and here was this so called Christian, who is even called "Pastor" in the church, preaching Christ with a whiskey bottle in one hand and a lottery ticket in the other. I was stunned at the contradiction.

I remember feeling, at times, that I was the only Muslim convert in the world. I suffered from a real sense of paranoia about what would happen to me if I was found out. I couldn't shake the fear that would creep up on me, telling me that I would be killed for my new-found faith.

Although I knew I couldn't expect my family to accept my Christianity, I did expect the situation in my school would be different. But instead of camaraderie in faith, surprisingly, I found apathy and worst, hostility, towards Christianity.

How could it be?

In fact, many of the kids I thought were Christians, weren't. They cussed. They drank. They stole. They took God's name in vain. They loved to talk about sin. Some were experimenting with drugs. Some were shameless in talking about their sexual exploits.

Is this Christianity?

I was beginning to understand the hypocrisy of calling one's self a Christian, and yet not having a real personal relationship with God that transforms us, and changes the way we live.

Lacking the spiritual support system I was accustomed to in Jerusalem, I found myself, at times, vacillating between my new found Christianity and my family's Islam.

Maybe I made a mistake leaving Islam? Maybe if I really learned Islam, and really gave myself whole heartedly to study the Koran, this phase would pass and I would be 100 percent committed to Islam?

These questions nagged at me. Sometimes I would lie awake at night thinking how I might be able to deepen my knowledge of Islam.

One day, I gathered my courage, and I asked my parents to send me to the Islamic school where I could study the Koran, but my parents refused because it was too expensive. Looking back, I see that was God's hand protecting me from falling back into the deception He saved me from.

I continued watching Christian television when I could at home, and I would often speak with a girl named Sarah at my high school. She had become my best friend. A strong believer, she would often remind me of God's unfailing love for me. She also seemed acutely aware of the struggle I was going through. She never condemned me. Instead, she seemed to understand my terror of being found out as a Christian. However, the contradiction I felt in myself was wearing on me; I felt phony. When I was with my family, I was playing along as if I was a Muslim. When I was with Christians, I was a Christian.

Was I denying Christ?

It was becoming unbearable.

Due, I suppose, to the helplessness I was feeling, a seed was planted in my mind and was starting to germinate: At a subconscious level, I think my next steps were being plotted. I knew eventually I'd have to make a decision for Jesus.

I knew I'd have to leave eventually, but I hadn't the slightest idea where I'd end up.

Graduation was nearing. May 2002. Following in my older brother

Nahel's footsteps, I decided to go to college. In addition to getting away from my family, college would provide me with a chance to practice my Christianity openly.

I started looking into different flight schools. I had always dreamed of being a pilot, and there was a school in southern Florida. Nahel told me not to worry about the financial aid situation. He said I just needed to go down to the school and talk to a financial aid counselor who would take care of everything.

At 17-years-old, I felt my dream of being an airplane pilot was close to being fulfilled. I would be a success, and my father, for the first time in my life, would be proud of me. I packed my bags, and I headed down to the Embry Riddle Aeronautical University in Daytona, Florida. It was three hours away from home.

The euphoria of actually being my own man began to sink in. I could hardly wait to get started on my pilot's license. The closer I got to the school, the greater my exhilaration. It felt like I was finally breaking free. I believed I was heading to a place where I could finally live my life as a Christian, without my family breathing down my neck.

Following my brothers advice, I immediately set up an appointment with the financial aid counselor. I told her my situation and about my desire to be enrolled at the college.

The counselor was kind, but adamant that the financial aid applications should have been completed at least six months in advance. There was no way that I could apply and get an answer in time for the upcoming semester. The hope I felt on my way down there was beginning to dissipate. I tried everything I knew to get my enrollment approved, but it was futile.

Blackness seemed to fall around me. I felt like such a fool.

Why didn't my brother explain this to me? Didn't he care if I began school on time? Why didn't I, myself, realize that this paperwork should have been in order prior to me heading down to the school?

I couldn't bear the thought of returning home to my family, having failed before even trying. I was so desperate to make it work; I spent hours with the guidance counselor to no avail.

By July 3, it was obvious that pilot school wasn't a viable option. I didn't have the energy to resist the tide of events that were swirling around me and threatening to swallow me up.

I called my father to tell him. His reply, as I expected, was that I return to Miami and work in the convenience store with my brothers. He was unbending.

I'd heard that tone of voice from him before, and I always obeyed. I feared my dad in an unhealthy way. He had total control of me, and of all my siblings. All he would have to do is look at me with a look of displeasure, and it would fill me with alarm. We were not allowed to question his authority. In Middle Eastern families, the authority structure is often rooted in an ancient patriarchal honor system. Any attempt to buck the system is met with fierce resistance.

This time, however, something inside of me was pulling me in a different direction. I couldn't obey this time.

The pilot school option, for all intents and purposes was gone, for now at least. In hindsight, I suppose the whole aspiration to go to school was really just a cover for my desire to leave home, and to live the life I knew I was called to live.

Pilot school or not, my longing to be my own man and to freely serve

Christ was still beating in my heart fervently. Though my family may not have realized it, I was different from them. I believed differently. I loved differently.

The fury in my father's voice mirrored the determination in my heart to break free. In those defining moments on the phone, I could tell that my father was beginning to realize that he had lost his control over me. The more the realization sank in, the stronger his insistence that I return home.

"Come home, work with your brothers in the store and never mind school!"

I struggled frantically to find the right words to say, but I soon understood that anything I said that contradicted his command would not make sense to him. Anything but strict, unconditional obedience was considered dishonoring to him. Those moments were so terrifying. Never in my life, had I thought to disobey and dishonor my father.

But as I spoke to him now, we were hundreds of miles apart. It didn't really matter that I argue or state my case. That seemed futile. But I did have to speak.

"Yaba, I can't come home."

His voice grew louder and angrier. He was beginning to curse.

I continued, "I can't come home because it's time for me to be my own man. I'm different, and I don't want to live the way my family is living."

The biggest issue facing me was Islam. I could not live that way. I only wanted freedom to live for Christ. I could not openly say that to my father. I didn't want to hurt him even more.

My father was livid by now. I had seen him like this so many times before. I wasn't surprised at his reaction but the difference was that, for the first time, I chose to have a say in my own life. I could not turn back despite the agony.

When he saw that he couldn't control me, my father used what was his usual last resort: threats.

He spoke the words I'll never forget, "Be home by 8 a.m. tomorrow morning, or you will never be a son in this family, or welcome in our house ever again."

In his typical rage, he handed the phone to my older brother who took over for him, cursing me, and commanding me to come back home. Then my brother slammed the phone down.

Silence.

In the tiny college dorm room, I sat alone. My ears were ringing. My heart was beating loudly. I wanted time to think of all that was happening, but there was no time. To get to Daytona from Miami, my father and brother would need three hours by car.

These three hours felt like my escape hatch. I had to make my decision. If I waited, they might come to get me, and take me back by force, since I was legally his dependent and still a minor under the age of 18.

Of all the steps I had taken in my life, up to this point, this one seemed to be the hardest. It was one I knew I would eventually have to take, but I didn't know how it would happen and what the fallout would be. It was like my personal Gethsemane moment when I had to make a final decision to follow God, no matter what the cost.

At 17 years old, I was insecure, completely dependent, and clueless. Yet, I was faced with having to make this enormous decision. I experienced what I call, the lesson of "The Imaginary Cuffs."

When you go to a circus you see exotic animals: elephants, camels etc. doing some pretty impressive tricks. Often times, they have on colorful costumes and other interesting adornments. When an elephant is being trained, it will have chains connected to the cuffs on his leg. The tug of the chain always pulls him back to his small circle. It limits his movement. There will come a point when the trainer detaches the chain, but leaves the metal cuff on his leg. Because the animal feels the cuff on his feet, the elephant thinks he is still connected to the chain. Those cuffs on his feet ensure that he stays within his allotted space. Pretty soon, the elephant forgets what it's like to be free. He just surrenders to the limitations imposed on him by the chain. So long as the cuffs are on him, he will always stay in his tiny circle and obediently perform his circus tricks.

My desire for religious freedom was contrasted with the fear of moving away from what I was accustomed to. The fear of the cost of freedom was like the chain that tugged me back to my family's home.

As I sat there in the tiny, dark college dorm room, I could taste spiritual freedom, and I knew it was worth whatever it cost, and the cost would be high.

To make it mine, I had to move quickly.

The only person I thought could help me was Isa. He was still in Jerusalem with his family, but was planning to come back to the U.S. in a few weeks. I called him, and he told me I could stay with his mother until he got back. He called his mother, Anne, who lived in Birmingham, Alabama, and told her that I was coming. I had spoken to his mother about a month earlier by phone and she, displaying typical Palestinian hospitality, invited me to come over to her house. Now, whether or not she meant it, I was about to take her up on that offer.

With all the energy I could muster, I got my things together and went over to the Greyhound bus station. I bought a one way ticket to Birmingham. As I stood in the station, I looked around. There were so many people coming and going. They were all focused, and hurrying to their respective destinations. I wondered if any of them was having a life crisis like the one I was going through at that moment.

Were they also running for their very lives? Were they embarking on a new life? Were they letting go of their pasts and facing a completely unknown future like I was?

The time came to board the bus; I stood in line behind the others, taking tiny steps until I reached my seat. The bus was full, and most of the people on it were not very friendly looking.

The man who sat next to me was probably in a similar situation as I am; at least, he looked like it. He wore raggedy clothes and had an unkempt beard.

Soon, I heard the sound of the hydraulic pump as it turned the bus door on its swivel. The door was closed, and we were on our way to Birmingham, Alabama.

So many times we go to church, and hear a message from heaven, that we disregard, or fail to cherish it, because things are going well in our lives, and we aren't aware of our need. Other times, we are desperate to hear from heaven. Any word from a stranger might do. Any lyrics from a song could help pull us through. Any street sign might help to point us in a direction.

I was desperate. I looked out the bus window as we pulled away from the station. To the right was a car lot. There were several navy blue Volkswagen Bugs lined up next to each other, but at the end of the row of navy blue buses, was a bright yellow one.

Through that line of Volkswagens, the voice inside spoke, "I called you to be different."

CHAPTER 4

Alabama

S teps are not all the same. Some steps go up, and some go down. Some go away from, and some go towards.

Steps are also distinguished by what motivates them. Some steps we take because we have no choice. People may push, or pull on us, to force us to take certain steps. Other steps, we take because we want to.

The Bible says the steps of a good man are ordered of the Lord.

Were all these steps I was taking of Him? Was He directing my steps which seemed to be leading me from the dark, and yet familiar, life I had always known to an uncertain future?

The 12-hour bus ride from Daytona Beach ended at the Birmingham, Alabama station. Whatever excitement I felt at the start of this journey was pretty much dissipated by the long, hot bus ride. My joy of being free was also constrained by my fear of not knowing how my family would react to my departure, or how Isa's family would react to me.

The only thing I felt sure of is that I could not back down. I could not go back to the life I was living before because I could not follow Islam.

Mechanically, I took the steps I knew I had to take. I got into a taxi cab that took me to the Bajalia's home. We stopped in front of the house. It was a typical middle class American home with a few distinguishing Middle Eastern features.

Stepping out of the taxi, I paid the driver, and turned to face the house. I took a few steps toward the house, and I stalled.

How could I be doing this? Could this be what God has for me?

I recounted for myself all my reasons for leaving my father's home in the first place. All those reasons, together, didn't equal the importance of my commitment to Christ. That was at the heart of my being here.

Step. Step.

It was late. I wondered if anyone could see me standing there in the street, eyeing the Bajalia's home. I took a few more steps and stopped.

Could I have stayed in Florida? Would my father have eventually accepted me as a Christian?

Imagining my father's reaction to my Christianity, and remembering the way he yelled at me on the phone, gave me a burst of motivation. I took several more steps towards the door, but I stopped again.

What will they think of me? Surely, they will think I'm crazy. Will they be scared of me?

The last thing I wanted was to scare them. But I felt I had no choice. I had nowhere else to go.

The steps got harder as I got closer to the house. It felt like I was dragging myself along in molasses, but I eventually made it. I planted my feet on the welcome mat.

Would that 'welcome' apply to me? I wondered.

Standing at the door, my mind flashed back to Isa's door in Jerusalem. I knocked on that door, and my life has never been the same.

What will this door mean?

That question was too big; I didn't have the energy, or desire, to ponder it. I needed some help, and if I didn't get some, I wasn't sure how I would make it.

I clinched my right fist, lifted it up to the door, hesitated, closed my eyes, and knocked softly. No answer. I did it again, only louder and harder.

An old woman came to the door. She had white hair and was very short. In a green floral print dress, she stood there looking at me strangely. Her eyes were Arab, for sure. I recognized Isa's family traits in her eyes.

She smiled kindly and ushered me into the house. She took me straight to the room where I would be sleeping. I put my things down and tried to relax. This was like my first smell of freedom. I tried to enjoy it. This was my first time out from under my father's shadow.

Her sympathetic eyes signaled an open heart. The food was amazing. A native of Ramallah, she knew all the recipes of my homeland. The smells wafting through the air created a sense of familiarity that I clung to, and longed to hold onto, but I felt uneasy as well. It didn't feel like home, and I soon understood that I wasn't wanted here.

Isa's two brothers, Samuel and Gerard, came to meet me. Like Isa, Samuel was legally blind. They came and listened to my story. They are a nominal Christian family, but my time in the U.S. had taught me that not everyone who calls themselves a Christian is really a born again believer.

Any hope of feeling at home was quickly dashed. Though the brothers allowed me to stay at their home, they were not welcoming. They made sure I felt like an intruder, an unwelcome guest. What really hurt was that I could empathize with their feelings.

They never met me before. They didn't know who I was, or what my story was. They didn't have anything to do with my predicament, so why should they be burdened with my presence after my fall out with my dad?

Even though the arrangement was only intended to last a few weeks until Isa got back, it was awkward, and extremely uncomfortable.

After a few days at Mrs. Bajalia's home, some of Isa's relatives, George and Janet Mobarak, came by the house. They professed their faith in Jesus and were true believers. We had a spiritual connection right away.

Aware of the way I felt, the Mobaraks offered to let me stay in their home until Isa arrived. I agreed. It was such a blessing to be with them. We had true Christian fellowship together.

They took me with them to the First Baptist Church of Hoover. For the first time, I was beginning to taste the freedom of religion which I sought. For me, that church was cutting edge. The love from the people and the fact that we could all celebrate and sing about our love for Jesus was so special. It was definitely a new experience for me, compared to the mosques I was accustomed to, which were usually very somber and anti social.

Through George and Janet, I experienced the love of Christ. It really felt like I was living a part of Jesus' promise, "If anyone leaves mother, father, brother, sister, homes or lands for My sake, he shall receive 100 fold in this life and then life eternal."

They opened their home, and far more importantly, their hearts to me. They were part of my 100-fold reward.

A few days later, Isa, Alene and Jarad returned from the Holy Land, and we picked them up from the airport and headed to their home in Maylene, Alabama. Their home was nice and quaint. It had all the necessities.

I shared a bedroom with Jarad who was 13 at the time.

That small room with the bunk beds would become my escape from reality. Inside that room, I could stay in bed, constantly listening to the radio. If I wasn't sleeping, I'd be in the kitchen looking for food.

The residue of my past, and the hope of living a Christian life, seemed to collide, creating a great struggle in my soul. I tried to fight it, but the clouds were too dark. If the darkness wasn't enough, the sun seemed to hide behind those clouds.

All I wanted to do was sleep all day long. I just wanted to hide under the covers where I could close out the world and forget all my troubles. At least, that's what I began to think.

My life had been so convoluted. I was born in New York, where my parents divorced. I was moved to the Holy Land, where I became a Christian, and then ended up coming back to Florida, where I was driven to leave my home and family to find freedom of religion. It was overwhelming to my young and immature soul. I was codependent upon my father and the family I had to leave behind. But I had also burned all my bridges. I felt there was nothing to go back to.

Now I felt alone in this really big, scary world. These Christians were so wonderful to take me in, and help me feel loved, but it felt like I was going through an identity crisis, not sure who I was, or what would become of me.

During that time, I also felt that I had to make an effort to show my dad that I still loved him. Each Saturday I would attempt to contact him by phone. For the six preceding days, I'd prepare myself psychologically for my father's reaction. From my end, I just wanted him to know that I wasn't out to cause him shame. Having a son change his religion is the greatest embarrassment to any Muslim family, and I knew that my family would be mocked for my decision. The last thing I wanted was to hurt my family, but at the same time, I could not deny Christ who had given me hope.

When Saturday rolled around, I would gather all my courage and nervously stand by the phone. I'd lift the speaker, and push the numbers. I had called the number so many times that I knew the pattern my father's phone number formed on the keypad without looking.

I'd listen patiently as my father's phone rang. With each ring, my heart would beat faster and harder. If he answered, I would say, "Yaba it's me Hazem."

Sometimes, upon hearing my voice, he would instantly hang up. Other times, he would pick up the phone, but not say a word. If he was alone, or had the energy to curse me out, he would. Sometimes, he would just command me to not call back. Other times, the phone would just ring and ring.

For six months, I went through this painful ritual every Saturday. I learned how to shield myself for his responses which were usually predictable.

Those days were so difficult. I literally had no energy to get out of bed. It took every ounce of motivation in my core to simply get up. It got to the point that I was averaging 12-15 hours of sleep a day and even that was never enough. My weight also got out of control. I weighed 225 pounds.

But one day, things changed.

I was watching a very interesting character on television. I remembered seeing him on TV when I lived in Israel. He was mysterious enough to me to grab my attention. His name was Benny Hinn. As I was watched him minister, I heard that familiar inner voice, "This is what I have called you to."

I knew that voice was not just my own. A very sobering feeling came over me. It was so real that it shook me to my core.

I remember thinking; I can barely get out of bed each day, never mind start ministering healing to other people.

Not knowing how to respond to the strange message, I did the only thing I knew to do: sleep.

I went back to bed, but something happened on the inside of me that I didn't quite understand. I kept thinking about the voice that had called me that day. At first, I consciously rejected it. I did not agree with it, and I did not receive it. As far as I was concerned, it was nothing more than a scary thought.

But the next morning when I woke up, it felt like there were rays of the sun breaking through the clouds. Light was filling the dark cavern of my soul. Something different was going on inside me. It was something I hadn't felt in a long, long time. I actually wanted to get out of bed.

I slowly started getting back on my feet. I got a job as a cashier at a Chinese restaurant, Yoe Express, in Homewood, Alabama. With some help from a very special loved one, I bought a car, a 1993 Chevy Lumina.

Spiritually, and emotionally, things really started looking up. I also took some concrete steps in my relationship with God. Within a month, I was baptized by Pastor Truett Murphy of the Living Word Church in Pelham, Alabama. This is now the Church of the Highlands Riverchase campus.

After a few months, Isa, Alene and Jarad had to go back to Israel. This was a stretching experience for me as they had been such a source of strength and encouragement to me.

There was a family in the church that asked me to move in with them. They welcomed me to stay with them. Being both very naïve and desperate for a place to stay, I took them up on their offer. But to say I was shocked by their lifestyle would be a gross under statement. Their home life was so different from what I saw in church.

After a few weeks in their home, I had to leave. I came home from work to find my clothes in big black plastic bags in the foyer. With no explanation, I was told to leave the house.

Yet again, I was being kicked out. Yet again, I was unwelcome. Yet again, I had nowhere to go.

That night, I slept in my Lumina. The disappointments of the preceding weeks and months could have been enough to drive me crazy. But deep in my heart was a flickering flame of the presence of the Holy Spirit that didn't go out. It kept me looking up in spite of everything I saw around me.

The next day I called one of Alene's daughters, Laura. When she heard what the family had done, she was upset and demanded that I come stay with her family in Decatur, Alabama which was about two hours north. She assured me that I could live with them for a few weeks until I found a place to stay. Being without options, and very grateful for her kindness, I went to Decatur.

The next Sunday, I attended an amazing church called Calvary Assembly of God in Decatur. Laura introduced me to the youth pastor Stan Rivers.

I still remember shaking Pastor Rivers' hand. He was a very sweet man about 35 to 40 years old. As he shook my hand, he said, "The Lord just spoke to me."

"What did the Lord say to you?" I asked.

"God spoke to me to pay for your scholarship to attend our Masters Commission program."

He was obviously busy, so I thanked him, and we made plans to reconnect later. I asked around about the program, and it sounded like a glass of cold, fresh water to my thirsty soul. I had had a traumatic past few years, in and out of peoples' houses. The thought of being set for the next year in that discipleship program, at a great church, was extremely appealing to me.

The Master's Commission Program was scheduled to start five months later. In the meantime, I had to find a job and a place to stay. Within a few days, I landed a job at Staples Copy Center in Decatur. The church helped me find an apartment with a couple of young men my age. They allowed me to stay in the living room. I had to sleep on the floor, but, in light of some of my other living situations, it felt like the lap of luxury.

As the time for the Masters Commission drew closer, I was getting more and more excited about the things of God. Attending church was so good for me, and I was so eager to learn the Bible. I had a plan, and I was growing in my relationship with God. As the weeks past, I was less and less interested in my job. The desire to be more involved in church was all consuming. I felt my job interfered with my church life.

In this time of uncertainty, I heard about a conference that was coming to our town. It was a "racial reconciliation" conference that was put on by some of the greatest speakers of our generation: Chuck Pierce, Dutch Sheets, James Goll and others. The conference was part of a 50 state tour to help undo some of the spiritual damage caused by racism.

I saw white preachers praying and repenting to the black people and vice versus. Native Americans were blessing the whites, and the whites were praying for them as well. It was so beautiful to see these acts of reconciliation around me. Having seen so much war and hatred between the Palestinians and the Israelis, I was excited when I saw a man there who was wearing a kipa, or yarmulke, which is a small circular head covering that Orthodox Jews wear. Having lived in Jerusalem, I often saw men wearing these head coverings. This man was on the other side of the sanctuary.

I thought since all these people are reconciling with each other, I might as well reconcile with this Jewish man. I began walking towards him, and as I did, he began to make his way to the back of the hall. I was losing sight of him since the place was crowded, but I felt the urge to do this. I ran towards him and finally caught up to him in the hallway. I was out of breath and trying to get my words together.

"Excuse me. Excuse me, Sir. Hi, my name is Hazem and I noticed that you are a Jew. I am a Palestinian and since all these people are reconciling with each other I just figured you and I should do the same. I am a follower of Jesus Christ, and He commands us to love our enemies, so here I am. I ask you for forgiveness for all the heartache my people have caused to you and your people."

This was the best way I could explain myself. At this point, it wasn't my intention to speak politics or discuss who is right and who is wrong. I just wanted to obey the words of Jesus. It was kind of awkward. We were complete strangers, and he was maybe twice my age.

After a short pause, I could tell he was moved by what I said.

"Welcome to the family of Yeshua and I, too, pray for your forgiveness and love despite our wars," he said. Then he hugged me and shook my hand. We parted and went our separate ways. What I did not know is that he was the assistant to one of the keynote speakers. His name was David. He told the speaker James Goll what I had said.

The conference leaders were so moved by what I did that I was asked to share my testimony. The next morning, I was brought up to the pulpit. They stood me in front of all these people. It was the first time I ever held a microphone in my hand. As I was stuttering my way through, I noticed all these best-selling authors and hugely respected men of the Western church world all around me, but who was holding the microphone that morning? Me: A confused Arab boy who just wanted to obey the words of Jesus.

I shared a few words and the crowd's reaction was amazing. Without even trying, and not even realizing it, I was doing the very thing that Voice had called me to do.

My participation in that conference opened a door that would lead to another stage in my life. The guest gospel singer, Karen Wheaton, was there with her praise and dance team, Chosen. Her dance team members were all dressed in black clothes.

After the service, Karen Wheaton walked up to me and invited me to her ministry center which is called The Ramp. Located a few hours away in Hamilton, Alabama, The Ramp was a worship center that Wheaton had founded in 1999. Some of my friends were planning to go there a few weeks later, and they asked me to go along.

When we got there, I was blown away. It was completely out of control. Had I been the driver, I would have left that place as fast as I could, but I wasn't, so I had to stay. I saw all these young people dancing profusely. They were bare-footed and swaying and spinning, jumping and shouting to loud worship songs. Many of them looked like hippies, and the music was so loud. It was just overload for someone like me, who felt stretched to merely clap my hands during a worship service in church.

When we did finally leave, I told my friends I never wanted to go back to that crazy place.

A few weeks later, I was told of another former Muslim who was at our church. His name was Khaleed, and he was the assistant to worship leader Eddie James. Meeting Khaleed was a breath of fresh air for me. I often thought I was the only former Muslim in the world. As ridiculous as this sounds to me now, I really felt that way.

When I met Khaleed, we immediately clicked. I grew in my relationships with both Khaleed and the worship leader, Eddie James. Khaleed was the first Arab American I met after coming to Decatur. At the time, I was trying to "un-Arabize" myself. I was so ready to leave my culture and my roots behind. In fact, I grew my hair out real long and curly, and pierced my ear, trying to look like I was a "normal" American.

When people would ask my name, if they were not paying attention, they would think I said my name was "Adam," since Hazem sounds like Adam. I really thought about changing my name. I wasn't able to change my name legally though because I was afraid that any legal maneuvers would be reported to my family, and they would find out where I was.

I didn't want anyone to know my address or location. As far as I was concerned, I was Adam. I was not Hazem. I wanted to run away from everything I considered Arab.

To be honest, I had been ashamed of my culture for many years. This was another thing my father was upset about. He knew I was ashamed of my culture. Not knowing how to deal with this issue, he would just get mad and yell at me, but my Heavenly Father knew how to deal with it.

One Sunday, I was attending a church for one of my first few visits there in a little town called Winfield. The name of the Church was called Faith Fellowship, and the pastor's name was Harry Saylor. This day, they had a guest speaker named Pat Shcatzline Jr. He was only there for a few services. During an altar call, at the end of one of the services, he said, "Whoever needs a touch from the Holy Spirit, come up."

I went up to the altar, and he started praying for me. He laid his hands on me, and then he abruptly took his hands off me. He opened his eyes, looked at me and said, "The Lord says to you, 'Stop running from your culture.'"

Instantly, something happened in my heart and mind that I still can't describe. The best way I can explain it is to say that Adam finally embraced Hazem. Upon hearing those words, years of shame, embarrassment and trauma broke off of me. For the first time in my life, I was proud to be Arab. From that moment, my love for my people has only grown. I am an Arab by blood, an American by birth, and a Christian by choice.

Not long after that, the Lord spoke to me again through another prophet. This time God dealt with the most intimate aspect of my identity: son ship. One problem that I feel is stalking this generation is the doubt of their legitimacy. Whether this is a result of careless and hasty words from parents, or the lack of fathers and mothers, it's a problem I have seen many times over.

It's not, however, a problem too big for God. As a matter of fact, He is the solution to it. Many times over, at the altars of prayer in many different churches, young people say things that reveal their emotional status. Many of these, with tears streaming down their faces, and voices crying from the depths of their souls, feel orphaned. Maybe their own parents made them feel unwelcome and rejected. For some, their parents bailed out. For others, the parents may have been physically present, but emotionally withdrawn, leaving the son or daughter with a huge void and a lot of rejection issues. This is all too familiar in our society unfortunately. In America, in spite of our incomparable prosperity, a healthy, vibrant home is hard to find. This cycle goes on, and the children grow into teens with this orphaned spirit. These teens grow into adults, and then they become parents, and the cycle repeats itself all over.

After years of living this way, I had a revelation that I didn't have to live orphan-spirited any longer. I had been praying about the situation with my own father. One morning, I started praying for his salvation. I fervently lifted up my prayers to God. A few hours after praying, I saw how my prayers were being undermined by doubts, as I allowed lies and fear to grip my mind.

A few days later, I was still in a battle in my mind. I was on my way to meet my ministry team. The only thing I knew to do was to be faithful to the ministry and preach by faith.

On the way there, I remember thinking vividly, Lord, I am going to minister, but the truth is I need ministry myself.

The service was good as the believers gathered that Sunday morning. After the service, a man who knew nothing of the battle that was raging on in my mind walked up to me. We shook hands and he said to me, "I have a Word from God for you."

I smiled at him even though skeptical thoughts shot through my mind. We walked away from the crowd to a quieter area in the back of the church.

Come on. Let's get this over with, I thought. It seemed so many people always had "a word" for me at that point.

Within seconds, my skepticism collapsed. His words pierced my heart like an arrow. Truly, it was a timely word from God, "In order for there to be an adoption, there must be a separation. Romans 8:15 is yours today. You are not an orphan, for God in heaven is your Father. For you have not received the spirit of fear; but you have received the Spirit of adoption, whereby you cry out to your Abba Father."

Although I still do get homesick sometimes, that man's words changed my life. From that day on, I have not felt the sting of rejection as it pertains to being separated from loved ones. My Heavenly Father has filled that void in my heart.

Have you received your Heavenly Father yet? Have you encountered the Father in your life or are you still orphan-spirited? You don't have to be fatherless any longer! What He did for me that Sunday, He will do for you, as well. That hurting child within you can finally crawl up on Daddy's lap, and you can grow into a healthy adult, leaving behind issues of rejection. Let them go. Be whole in your inner person. No longer be haunted! God loves all His creation equally. Romans 8:15 can be yours as well, if you receive it today, into your heart, by faith. For those of us who have felt like we are fatherless, there's no greater joy than to know that He is a father to the fatherless.

One day I overheard Khaleed say that Eddie needed someone to answer the office phone, reply to e-mails, and take care of simple office work. This was my first opportunity to leave my secular job and be involved in the ministry. After working with them a few weeks, Eddie asked me to go with him to Hamilton, Alabama.

I recalled the nightmarish experience I had when I first went to Hamilton. To my shock, it turned out that Eddie was a frequent guest worship leader there at The Ramp. From then on, I found myself making weekly trips to the very place to which I swore I would never return. After three visits to the Ramp, and meeting the people there, I began to understand the reason for their extravagant worship. They sincerely loved Jesus with all their hearts;

that was a good enough reason for me.

After a while, Karen told me she felt that God laid it on her heart that I should be traveling with her ministry team.

Immediately, I told her, "Oh, well, God spoke to Mr. Rivers and I'm going to start Master's Commission."

She suggested that I do what I felt was God's will.

Khaleed, who was a strong supporter of The Ramp, really urged me to think about what I was going to do. We would have arguments at times because he believed that I was to be with Karen. Deep inside, I knew it was a good idea, but the insecure, paranoid part of me wanted to stay in an obscure little Alabama town where I would be safely hidden. I didn't want to be moving around to all these big churches to where I might even be on TV.

I fought the idea of joining Karen's team as long as I could. I was completely focused on starting Master's Commission. But as the time drew closer, I would have a queasy feeling each time I thought of starting the Master's Commission Program.

I waited till the end of the 5 month period and asked for a meeting with Pastor Rivers. Confused, insecure, and not wanting to hurt his feelings, I walked into his office and told him that I no longer had peace about doing Master's Commission. It was so hard to look at him and tell him those words. A few months before, when I was in a desperate situation, he boldly said "God spoke to me." He was so sure God spoke to him that he put down $5,000 of his own money to pay for my Master's Commission tuition. And now, I had to tell him I couldn't do what he thought was God's will.

He said to me, "Son, we both can't be hearing God. Now, either I'm missing God or you're missing God," insinuating, of course, that I was missing God.

I assured him that I was appreciative and thankful for his commitment to doing what he thought was God's will, but that I had to follow what God was telling me to do. I walked out of that office, and I was Hamilton, Alabama bound.

Chapter 5

Those who wait...

By this stage in my life, I was adept at moving around. From the crowded streets of Brooklyn to the contentious, holy mountains of Jerusalem; from the idyllic world of South Florida to the, at times, inhospitable receptions encountered in Alabama, my life seemed to take on its own momentum. It was almost as if an invisible Hand was guiding me.

So often, along this journey, I felt unwanted and unwelcome. Many times, I felt like I was imposing on others, but something inside propelled me. I knew I had had an encounter with God, and a calling was birthed in me from that encounter. I knew I had to give myself to this passion that burned inside my heart.

In spite of all the uncertainty that accompanied these previous months and years, I could not deny the fingerprints of God all along this journey. He was leading me. At times, this leading seemed mysterious. But other times, God's leading was so blatant that I was awestruck at His care. In addition to leading me, He would also, often confirm that I was on the right path.

The inner voice of the Holy Spirit was so clear at times. Sometimes, I was so eager to follow His commands; other times, less so, but one of the great secrets I learned along the way is that He is truly a Friend who sticks closer than a brother. He is true to His promise to be with me in all my trials, to guide me along the way, and to never leave or forsake me.

One of the steps in my journey that brought me particular joy was moving to Hamilton. It was exactly what my rattled soul needed to begin to heal. From the instability and uncertainty of the previous years, Hamilton was a place where I could actually begin to feel grounded emotionally, psychologically and spiritually.

A town of about 5,000 people, Hamilton had only six streetlights. In this peaceful haven, I began to grow in my relationship with God and in my relationships with other believers. For once, I didn't feel I had to look over my shoulder in fear of who might be following me. I didn't have to fret about where I was going to sleep that night.

It was like a special grace from the Father, the Giver of all good and perfect gifts.

Karen Wheaton was like a mother to those of us on the ministry team. A well-known and respected Gospel singer, she opened many doors for us to minister in the U.S. and around the world.

On an almost weekly basis, we would minister in different churches. I soon became part of the ministry leadership team and was often called on to preach and share during our services. I was learning to flow with the Holy Spirit, and the gifts of the Spirit were beginning to manifest in my life. It was an exciting time of discovery for me. It was almost like a crash course in supernatural and international ministry. It also meant I was often on stages, behind pulpits and on television.

With all the exciting changes in my life and the whirlwind pace of the ministry, Hamilton became a peculiar treasure. It was the eye of the storm, a quaint and peaceful place, where my soul was renewed. It provided the perfect balance I needed in my hectic life.

During my first month in Hamilton, I stayed in a small retirement home that was turned into a motel. The room itself was not very pleasant, but for the time being it was mine! The hospital scents still lingered, but I didn't care.

What I didn't know was that, a few months earlier, Pastor Harry Saylor of Faith Fellowship Church and his wife Sandra had been in a season of intercession, specifically burdened to pray for "the seed of Ishmael."

The Lord told Pastor Saylor to open his basement apartment to me. After one month at the retirement home, I moved into the Saylors' comfortably refurbished basement-apartment. I so longed for some stability in my life at this point; I needed to have a place I could call "home."

The Lord blessed me in this season with this wonderful pastor and his family. It's one thing to respect someone when you first meet them, but it's a whole other story when you can live in that person's home for two years, and the respect just grows. That's what happened with the Saylors.

Pastor Saylor had his priorities right in life. He loved his family and he led them as a true role model. He is the closest thing to a godly example of fatherhood that I have ever experienced. The Lord blessed me so many times through this relationship. From day one, Harry Saylor and his family became the oak trees I could always rely on in my life. It was during my time with Pastor and Mrs. Saylor that I would find my place and know what it means to feel at home.

It was no surprise to the either of them that a young man, of the "seed of Ishmael," would be placed in their home. I faithfully attended their church, Faith Fellowship, when I wasn't on the road with the team.

Most weekends, I'd travel to churches around the country and the world. I was part of Karen Wheaton's ministerial team, "Chosen," that backed her up during her concerts. It was an unexpected and amazing blessing in my life.

It was during a performance, at an Atlanta TBN Praise-a-Thon in 2003, that God would introduce me to another power couple that would become a great blessing, and be so instrumental in my life as a Christian, Paul and Jan Crouch.

As Karen sang, we performed our dance routine behind her. In between songs, I would look over the huge, exuberant audience. It was interesting to be in front of them with all the camera equipment and bright lights focused on us. These were becoming regular fixtures in my life, even though, at this stage in my life, I was still dealing with my paranoia of being found out.

At one of the Praise-a-thon services, I felt a sense of panic in my heart. It was like the tension I felt back in Jerusalem when God told me to give back the Bible I had hidden under my bed.

That same Voice said to me, "Get ready."

Get ready for what? I wondered.

I knew something was going to happen that night, but I had no idea what.

At this point in the service, Pastor Jentzen Franklin was preaching. His sermon was about the patriarch Joseph. Pastor Jentzen described the way Joseph's brothers had sold him to the Ishmaelites, and he warned of the danger of "selling our callings and futures to the Ishmaelites." As an Arab, I knew that I was an Ishmaelite, but I understood that he was talking about a spiritual principle.

The enthusiastic crowd was joyfully absorbing all of the significant points from Pastor Jentzen's message. People were clapping, shouting, and running the aisles; and the organ was playing so vigorously. It was pretty rowdy, but the anointing was so powerful.

As we were watching from behind, all of a sudden, Pastor Jentzen looked at Karen Wheaton and said, "Karen, I feel you have something to say from the Holy Spirit."

Karen walked right over to me and took my hand; she pulled me out of the group of dancers. She put me front and center, before the whole world.

She then placed a microphone in my hand and said, "Hazem! Here is a son of Ishmael."

There I was again, standing in the presence of some of the greatest preachers in the Western world. And again, I had the microphone in my hand, and the eyes of everyone in the hall, and the millions of people watching from their homes, were on me.

I hesitated, stuttered a few words, and then a prayer flowed out. The audience applauded enthusiastically, and I was overwhelmed by their reaction and the love I felt from them and from the ministry team. I was somewhat distressed, though, that God would orchestrate such an event and not give me more than a few moments warning.

I remember trying to avoid the glare of the cameras by hanging my head down. The director however was adamant. He had the camera man positioned on the ground right in front of me looking up.

At that point, I knew there was no turning back.

Then, Jan Crouch, who was standing with the group of ministers, walked over to me and took a silver ring off of one of her fingers. In front of everyone, she gave it to me. Her eyes were moist with tears.

I was overwhelmed. Unsure what this all meant, I just took the ring, put it in on my finger, and cherished it.

After that Praise-a-thon, I returned to Hamilton and continued as before in my ministry with Karen. It was during this time that I was really hoping for a chance to meet the man, whose program God used to pull me out of my depression a few years earlier, Benny Hinn.

I was so longing to meet the man who had broken through so many of the same cultural barriers I was now facing. He not only broke through, but he thrived doing so. For the whole year of 2003, I was hoping to meet him.

In December 2003, the Holy Spirit began to stir me in another way. As I was praying, I felt the Lord clearly telling me to go visit my father. I knew exactly why God wanted me to go at this time. I later found out that my father was about to go on his second pilgrimage to Mecca and would be leaving in a few weeks.

Pilgrimage to Mecca is one of the five pillars of Islam, along with prayer; fasting for the month of Ramadan; giving alms to the poor and saying the creed, declaring that "There is no God but Allah and Mohammed is his messenger." All Muslims, who are able, are expected to make the pilgrimage to Mecca at least once in their lifetime. The pilgrimage is attended by several rituals, including the stoning the devil at Jabal Arafat; visiting the tomb of Mohammed in Medina and walking seven times around the black cube, the Ka'aba, and kissing the sacred stone. Muslims believe that through these rituals, they will attain forgiveness for their sins and will be granted a new beginning.

My father was already a Hajj, since he had made the pilgrimage previously, but as is often the case, Muslims go back to Mecca several times to wash away their sins.

The reason, this would have been an opportune time to visit my father is that Muslims are supposed to try to get their homes in order, and to make their relationships right, before going to Mecca.

Surely, my father would want to make up with me and to reconcile so that his pilgrimage would not be wasted.

I felt certain that God was telling me to make this visit but, in all honesty, the last thing I wanted in my life was drama. Going to see my father was likely be extremely confrontational.

I started to remember how he used to yell at me and curse me. I remembered how he would hang up the phone on me. I remembered how he used to threaten me, and how he told me to never return to the house.

I didn't want to go through this pain and anxiety again. I had experienced enough rejection from him, but the voice of the Spirit was persistent in my heart, "Go see your father."

After much inner struggle, I agreed, but I put a challenge before God. I committed to going to see my father only if God would make a way for me and pay for the tickets.

It was more like; I doubt this will happen, so I'm off the hook.

About five hours after that prayer, I got a phone call.

"Please hold for Mrs. Jan Crouch," a voice on the other end said.

Jan Crouch? Why was she calling me? The last time I saw her was in the spring and now it was December.

Then she spoke, "Hazem, how are you honey? We were just wondering if you would be interested in attending a Benny Hinn crusade with us in Costa Rica?"

I was so amazed. I really wanted to meet Benny Hinn. I was a little sad that I had missed his last crusade, and now the Lord was going to give me another chance to meet him with Paul and Jan Crouch.

But, wait, that wasn't all. On our way back from Costa Rica, the Crouches were going to spend a week at the Miami TBN station which is very close to Fort Lauderdale where my father lived. It was an immediate answer to my challenge. In fact, the TBN studio is in Pembroke Park, and my father's home is in the nearby Pembroke Pines.

My jaw dropped in amazement. God answered my prayer. I was going to see both Benny Hinn and my father.

God took the willingness of my heart, and opened the door for me to go with people who would surely be able to introduce me to Benny Hinn.

In a few weeks, we flew down to Costa Rica. It was a huge venue and tens of thousands of people were there. I was so excited to see what God was going to do that night, and I was so overjoyed at the prospect of actually meeting Benny Hinn, the man whose anointing pulled me out of a long slump in my life.

Then it came, the moment I had waited for, for so long. Back stage, before the conference, I stood with all these prominent preachers.

Dr. Crouch took me and introduced me to Pastor Hinn, "Benny, I want you to meet my key to the Middle East."

When I heard those words, I thought to myself, what is he talking about? I'm just me. I'm surely not a key to the Middle East.

Pastor Benny was very cordial and nice. But I was very nervous as I realized that before me stood men whose ministries were touching more lives than almost anyone else on earth.

In his deep, dramatic voice, Pastor Benny said to me in my own Palestinian dialect of Arabic, "So Hazem, your family is still Muslim and you're the only believer in the house, huh?"

I was so nervous that I wasn't able to think straight and instead of answering in Arabic, I blurted out, "Si Senor!"

I was so embarrassed, but it was so funny as well, and we all shared a laugh over it.

During this trip, I really hit it off well with Paul and Jan Crouch. I saw how tears would roll down Dr. Crouch's face as we discussed the needs of the Arabic people to hear the gospel. Dr. Crouch was already thinking of starting the Healing Channel, an all Arabic-language Christian channel for TBN that would broadcast all over the Arab world.

After the powerful crusade in Costa Rica, we returned to the TBN studio in Florida for the second reason for my trip – to meet with my father. I spent the night at the home of a TBN worker. He had a fold out sofa bed in his living room, and that is where I slept.

As I tried to sleep that night, my mind was filled with thoughts of what might happen the next day when I actually saw my father. Just a few years before, I defied his command and went to Alabama. For months, I tried to reconnect with him by phone, but he consistently and persistently rejected me. The whole time of my excursion away from home, I felt the dread of being found out, or being kidnapped, or maybe even worse, if my family knew where I was.

All these thoughts filled my mind as I drifted into slumber. Suddenly, I felt myself paralyzed. I could think clearly, but I couldn't move my body. I was alert, and I could even hear the TV from the next room. I was conscious, but immobile.

Then, I heard what sounded like a rattling of metal. It sounded like swords and shields clashing against each other in battle. It was all happening right around the sofa bed. The first time the metal clashed, I could actually feel it in my body. Then it happened again. I tried to yell, or say something, but I couldn't make a sound. I had no voice. Finally, when I felt the third and hardest blow, I remember thinking the Name "Jesus." As soon as I thought of His name, I was back to normal. I could move and speak again. I knew that I had just been given a window into the spiritual battle that awaited me the next day when I went to see my father.

When morning came, I took a shower, got dressed, and set out to see my father. The sense of uncertainty was familiar to me by now. As I got closer to the house I used to live in, I felt both a sense of dread and of emptiness. I knew I couldn't rely on my emotions to pull me through this test. The only lifeline I felt I could hold onto was the assurance that God wanted me to be here. God opened the door through the Crouch's for me to; first, meet Benny Hinn, and, then, to come back to this place to meet my father.

Getting out of the car, I walked towards the house. The closer I got, the stronger my apprehension. I had a strong urge to run away.

What if all my brothers attack me, and overpower me?

Step, step.

What if they hurt me?

Step.

Finally, I just allowed the events to dictate themselves; I surrendered to what I knew was God's will. Unannounced, I walked into the house and stood in the foyer area by the front door. I saw my dad walking by. He was on the phone talking.

As he walked by, he saw me standing there. He did a double take, and hung up the phone. As I expected, he flew into a rage. His words were like knives hitting me in my heart. His fury was tangible.

Fortunately, I wasn't harmed physically. I think the surprise factor was so great because he didn't have time to do anything beside yell and threaten me. My step-mother, brothers and sisters all were trying to get him to calm down. After he was done yelling at me, he turned on all of them as well.

In an uncontrollable rage, he stormed out the door, "I'm going to leave this house, and be back very, very soon. If you are here when I come back, you will be hurt."

I was trembling inside and out. My knees were shaking. I hurriedly got up and left the house. I went back to the Crouch's home and told them what happened. They were very sympathetic and supportive.

CHAPTER 6

When Growing Together Means Growing Apart

Things were so out of control in my personal life, the only thing I knew to do was to take one day at a time, one step at a time.

Shortly after this encounter with my father, I was asked to help with the youth and young adult service at a church in Tennessee. I had spoken at the church, and I knew that the pastors were very sincere and had great zeal in their hearts. Most of the 100 or so members of the church had a passion for the gospel. That was very evident.

I really felt I needed to take another step towards what God had called me to, and this was the door; I felt God had opened it for me. After about six months, the church was experiencing extraordinary things. From a handful of students, the youth group grew to an average attendance of about 400-450 young people from the local area. The population of the town was only 30,000 so we were amazed at the exponential growth we started seeing in a town of that size. God was doing mighty things in our meetings. Dynamic worship encounters, healings, and Holy Spirit outpourings had become regular occurrences. God was showing up! It was a precious lesson I would never forget.

An inescapable part of the Christian life is conflict. Jesus said that in the world we would have tribulation. Sometimes this conflict is with the world, the devil, and the flesh. But, if we are to be completely honest, we have to admit that at times, it is with other believers.

The conflict may be the result of sin. Sometimes it's the result of pride. Sometimes it's simply the result of misunderstandings or disagreements.

With each new step I took in the Lord, I found the potential for and, at times, the actual presence of conflict. Conflict isn't always bad. Paul and Barnabas had a conflict that helped to reshape the direction of their ministries.

As a new believer, I was thrust into the limelight of international ministry. I quickly rose through the ranks and learned the ropes of the ministry world, but there was one test I took over and over again: learning whether to obey the voice of God or the voices of those around me.

Having come from a controlling family with its strict Middle Eastern authoritarian structure, I knew what it was like to be under what may be considered, abusive control. People who are raised in this type of family often adapt easily to other overly controlling situations.

In the ministry world, there is potential for these same kinds of authority abuse. As a believer, I place great value on the authority structure of the church. Scripture says that Jesus is the Head of the Church and that He is the One who is building the church. It is built on the teachings of the Apostles who were ordained of God. Jesus, then, gave the Church the five-fold ministry: apostles, prophets, evangelists, pastors and teachers to help mature, direct and protect the flock of God from deceptions and dangers of the world.

No church or ministry is perfect; there are always problems and the potential for mistakes. While the authority structure is of God, which means we can base our lives upon it, problems can arise when this divinely instituted structure is placed into human stewardship.

The Apostle Peter says, "Church leaders, I am writing to encourage you. I too am a leader, as well as a witness, to Christ's suffering, and I will share in his glory when it is shown to us. Just as shepherds watch over their sheep, you must watch over everyone God has placed in your care. Do it willingly in order to please God, and not simply because you think you must. Let it be something you want to do, instead of something you do merely to make money. Don't be bossy to those people who are in your care, but set an example for them. Then when Christ the Chief Shepherd returns, you will be given a crown that will never lose its glory."

When a ministry is overbearing, people can become overly dependent on their leaders. Rather than teaching people to hear, and follow, the voice of the Holy Spirit for themselves, those leaders teach the flock to depend on them. This can often lead to "shepherding" – where leaders control all aspects of the lives of their flock. Some of the words that float around this type of ministry are fathering, submission, rebellion, and dis-fellowship.

If we've been raised in this type of a family or church, it can be hard for us to trust the leading of the Holy Spirit, especially if we feel that God is leading us in a direction different than the ones our leaders want.

The first time I really fought this battle was that day in flight school in Florida. My father was commanding me in that tone of voice I knew, dreaded and always obeyed. My spirit knew that God was calling me onward. The road I was to walk was different and, if I wanted it, I had to forsake all and follow the Voice of the Holy Spirit. As painful as it was, I made that break and have never regretted it.

That happened with me again when the youth pastor felt God told him I was to go to Master's Commission. At first, I could barely contain my excitement at the prospect of joining that discipleship program but then the Holy Spirit began to beckon me in a different direction.

One of the big obstacles to obeying God is that pesky, all-consuming desire to not hurt others' feelings. With the instance of this youth pastor, the pressure was compounded by the fact that he had offered to pay $5,000 for my Master's Commission training, and he was convinced that he had heard from God about making this enormous investment in the life of a young man he had never met before.

But in my heart, the Holy Spirit was calling me in a different direction. Unfortunately, for this youth pastor and me, it came to a head as we sat facing each other. It was so hard to disappoint him and tell him I didn't believe what he was offering me was God's choice for my life, but if I didn't obey the Voice of the Holy Spirit, I would have missed the other opportunities that God had in store for me.

After several months as the Youth Leader, the Lord led me to work with the Altar Time ministry also there in Tennessee. I really grew in the Lord and learned how to flow with the Spirit and work with others during my time there. I was outspoken and very visible in the ministry which had both an evangelical and pastoral component.

God really blessed me in those early days as we travelled and ministered all over Tennessee. In fact, it was during my time spent at Altar Time that God began to deal with some of the wounds of my past.

At Grace Fellowship in Humbuck, Tennessee, as was often the case, I was asked to share my testimony. I described how I was born and raised in Brooklyn, and how my mother had left our family. I shared how we moved to Jerusalem where I met Isa and Alene, and how I got saved out of Islam.

A few days later, an elderly Egyptian woman named Samia from that church called me.

She asked me a question I never thought about before, "Have you forgiven your mother?"

I told Samia I didn't have any bad feelings towards my mother, but that wasn't enough for her. She told me that I was in sin if I didn't try to reconcile with my mother. I wasn't averse to the idea of reconciling with my mother, but I just never thought about it before, and my mother had never made any gestures towards reconciling with me.

I was taken aback by Samia's words, but at the same time, I didn't want to miss what God might want to do through this encounter. I hung up the phone and was a little confused. I hadn't harbored any anger or unforgiveness towards my mother, at least not that I knew of.

I prayed, "Lord, You know my heart. If You want me to find her, help me please."

Exactly three days later, out of the blue, my biological mother called. She wanted to meet with me. I called Samia to tell her about the call, and she told me I could meet with my mother at her house in Indianapolis on my 21st birthday.

A few days later, we met. I wasn't sure what to expect.

Would it be a dramatic emotional encounter like I'd seen in the movies? Would my mother break down and beg for forgiveness?

Sitting together in that living room was extremely awkward. Within a few moments, I understood that this wasn't going to be dramatic or emotional. Of course, I recognized her, and remembered some of her mannerisms, but I was so young when she left, and it had been more than 15 years since I'd seen or spoken to her.

We avoided some of the hot button issues that could have derailed our first encounter: Why she left; why she didn't attempt to contact me?

Rather than mother and son, it felt like we were two strangers getting to know each other.

Within a few minutes, I understood that there was a role reversal. I wasn't there to find healing for what I went through so many years ago. Rather, I was there to try to help her find the One Who had changed my life - Jesus. I told her how I had become a Christian and was involved in the ministry. Even though she is Muslim, her reaction was far more receptive than anyone else in my family. I even got to share with her the story of the Samaritan Woman. I told her how Jesus had accepted her and forgave her.

She listened and even seemed genuinely interested. I think that was all I could expect from that meeting. At least I did what I had to do to reach out to my mom and to seek reconciliation. Since then, we have been in regular contact. She has not yet received the Lord, but the communication lines are open between us.

When I returned to the ministry center in Tennessee, I felt the Holy Spirit tugging at my heart again. He was calling me into a deeper walk that necessitated a new direction. This is where one of the greatest conflicts I had ever experienced arose.

Altar Times Ministry was solid and had a deep grounding in God's word, but I felt there was an over emphasis on our dependency on our leaders to hear from God for us.

Our leaders were involved in all aspects of our lives, personal and spiritual. We couldn't even go out on a date without their approval. We knew that the leaders heard from God and we came to rely on their ability to hear to the point of neglecting our own responsibility to learn to hear from God for ourselves.

I found it bearable to live under this type of authority until the Holy Spirit started leading me in a different direction. Until that point, I wasn't aware of how much control was exerted on my life. I knew, at once, God wanted me to leave.

In order to leave however, I had to deal with one of the scariest tools in the "shepherding" bag: control. If someone believes God is leading them in a direction that doesn't comply with the leaders' wishes, they could be made to believe they are disobeying not just the leaders, but God. This is what happened to me.

When I finally worked up the courage to tell the leaders that God wanted me to move on, the director, Tom Angles, asked me, "Do you think God will speak to me about it?"

I said, "Sure."

Although I knew in my heart what God wanted from me, I waited and waited for Tom to hear from God. Nine months passed, and I still hadn't heard anything from Tom.

The pressure inside me grew so strong that, after the nine months, I consecrated a time of prayer and fasting that lasted two weeks. I closed myself off in my apartment and sought God's face about what I should do and what I should say. I felt that God told me to say, "Tom and the ministry team are not in agreement with me about my decision, but this is what I believe God wants me to do.

As I sought God's direction, I was also led to read a set of scriptures a man had given me after a church service many months earlier. In my rush, I just took the verses and stuffed them in my Bible, thinking I'd come back to them at some later date. Well, this was that later date. I was desperate to hear from God. I sat and read each one.

Putting all these verses together, this is what those verses said, and if ever I received a word from the Lord, this was it!

"Thus saith the Lord: Go in peace for the Lord's approval is upon your journey. The Lord Himself will fight for you, for He is a mighty warrior. The time has come for all the prophecies to be fulfilled. No more delay."

It was comical to me how The Lord would use the words that someone gave me so long ago to guide me at this critical juncture in my life. The words seemed to speak to my heart, and gave me the courage and impetus to go and tell the leaders, once and for all, that I was leaving.

The next day, I walked into the ministry center. Everyone was friendly that day and seemed pleased to see me. I went over to Tom's office and approached his desk. He was sitting smiling at me and asked, "Well have you made your decision?"

"Yes, and I am leaving," I told him. "I want to go to Bible school and learn the Word of God."

He seemed stunned, initially. He told me that I needed to go back, and pray more about it. So, again, I went home and did as he said. As I started to pray, I fell asleep and I had a dream which confirmed that my instructions were from the Lord. Through the dream, I understood that I was engaged in a spiritual battle.

That night, I went back to the center. Tom was gathered with all the ministry team members. He was telling them to beware of the enemy's voice. I later found out that they were talking about me.

After that meeting, Tom took me back to the office, and he told me that if I left, the umbrella of God's protection would come off my life. I was shaken. I could feel the blood rushing through my head at his words. The pushback was furious.

I told him how I had a great desire to study God's word. I knew God had great things for me in the future, but I had to lay the groundwork and learn the Bible better. He was unmoved.

I had to make my decision to leave whether he agreed or not. He didn't. Sometimes, to follow God, you have to break free of the expectations of man no matter how well-meaning those expectations may be.

As I sat in the office with Tom, he told me that I was missing God's best for my life. It was blatant manipulation and control, the likes of which I had never seen. I knew it was my time to go, but he and some of the others disagreed. Six of my seven spiritual mentors in the ministry agreed with me that it was time for me to leave. But the seventh person, Tom, disagreed. It got so severe that I was threatened that I would be dis-fellowshipped. If I told people that God was telling me to leave against Tom's wishes, I would be dis-fellowshipped. It was a nightmare.

The mere word, dis-fellowshipped, had such a terrifying connotation. The Apostle Paul used this as punishment for heretics. For my decision, I felt I was being treated as though I was a heretic.

Another member of the ministry even told me that I was a Dimas, a man whom Paul said was a self-seeker, who always wanted to be "first." But the more pressure I felt coming against me, the surer I became that I had to go. The more I saw the control being exerted by the ministry to keep me from leaving, the more I knew I had to leave, or I would forever be a pawn in someone else's game.

What made it even harder to leave was the fact that I had worked so hard with this ministry. I, instantly, felt that deep sense of loss; grief. Tom's reaction, I dare say, was even more painful than what I had heard from my father when I told him I would not be returning home from flight school. I didn't even weep when my father blew up at me, but at Tom's words, I cried like a baby. Tom and the others, however, were completely unmoved by my tears.

As I walked out of the office that day, my face was flush; my head was hanging down; and I was barely able to look up at the other team members who were watching. My decision was my own. I didn't want to negatively impact the ministry, and I didn't want the responsibility of causing anyone else to leave it. I believed with my whole heart that I was doing what the Holy Spirit wanted of me, but it was a lonely road. For those few hours, I repeatedly second guessed myself.

Am I doing the right thing? Did I misread God's Voice? Was I being unfair to the ministry? Who am I to go up against such a great ministry?

Sometimes I think it is better not to second-guess yourself too much. It was terrifying to think that after I had given up my life in Islam, with my family, to follow Jesus Christ, that I would be cut off, or, as Tom said, "dis-fellowshipped."

All of the words I had heard those last few days with Tom left me literally reeling inside. I went to my apartment and felt so alone and hopeless.

It was hard to close my eyes and sleep.

What more could happen that day? What else might happen as I slept?

It felt like a whirlpool that was closing in around me at a furious speed. I couldn't slow it down or pull out of it.

In times like those, I learned to hold on to the strongest lifeline I have inside of myself: God's promises. The guilt and condemnation swirl around you, trying to pull you under. If you allow it, it could drag you to the center and overwhelm you.

God's words became my lifeline. My experiences with God in the past become a precious source of assurance. He, Who began a good work in me, would complete it.

David said in Psalm 63, "I think about you before I go to sleep, and my thoughts turn to you during the night. You have helped me, and I sing happy songs in the shadow of your wings. I stay close to you, and your powerful arm supports me."

As the hours passed, I fell in and out of sleep. Each time I'd awake, I'd find a new pocket of strength, but then the dark thoughts of all that happened would start swirling in around me again. It got to the point that I didn't want anything to do with ministry. I consciously laid it down because of all that had transpired. As far as I was concerned, that night, I laid everything down. I was done with ministry.

I even considered going back to Florida to be with my family. Maybe I'd go back to flight school and continue on the path that I started before I left my family. I wasn't even interested in going to Bible school anymore.

The next day, a friend of mine, Suzy, came over. She knew all that had happened. She looked at me, and I was comforted to know that she understood how I was feeling. She took me to her parents' house just to get me into a new atmosphere.

We sat down together in the living room and started watching television. I told her to turn it on to TBN. To my surprise, a friend of mine, Rich Wilkerson, was preaching. The anointing on him was so powerful. I felt it fill the living room where we sat.

At that moment, he looked right into the camera and said, "The Lord sent me here to TELL you something. You're a young person watching and you're about to give up but God wants you to know that you are not a quitter."

My ears perked up. I could feel the anointing as he spoke.

He pointed his finger right at the camera and continued, "I want you to know that you are like a Gideon, but you are not a quitter. Your family doesn't look like my family, and my family doesn't look like your family. My family is all preachers but your family is different."

I felt like he was speaking directly to me.

I asked Suzy, and some of the others, if those words ministered to them, but she said, "Hazem, those words are for you."

The overwhelming grief of the last 24 hours just dissipated. That one moment of watching TBN changed my direction. I was no longer thinking of going back to Florida. In spite of all the confusion of the past months and years, I felt a new sense of direction and hope. I was reminded again that God was working in my life and that I didn't need to look back. I could just continue taking the steps I knew God wanted of me. I needed to trust the unction of the Holy Spirit which was leading me.

I registered at International House of Prayer (IHOP) in Kansas City which is what I had been planning to do all along. Although it is a two-year program, I stayed at IHOP from 2008-2009. It was an amazing experience, almost like a modern day monastery. In addition to the educational aspect of the ministry, we were required to spend four hours a day in prayer. This was a great time of learning to experience God in my prayer life.

After my first year at IHOP, I started thinking about a career and planning for my future. Several opportunities presented themselves to me, but I felt most drawn to complete my pilot's license. That's what I always dreamed of doing, and for the time being, it seemed like the best move.

In 2009, I went back to Florida to start flight school to get my private license. As far back as I could remember, I wanted to get a pilot's license. It was my greatest "career" goal which is what made the whole experience of going back to Florida so strange. I was finally doing what I had wanted all these years but when I finally went, I was so miserable.

In those early days of flight school, I realized that the only reason I wanted to be a pilot was because my father used to taunt me about being "worthless." He said I would never amount to anything. When I told him I wanted to be a pilot he said I would never be a pilot because I was a failure. His taunts and mocking words drove me to prove him wrong.

Subconsciously, I was here at this pilot school, not because I really wanted to be here, but because I was trying to disprove my father. I had to show him I wasn't a failure. It didn't take long for me to find out that it wasn't what God wanted, and it wasn't what I wanted, either.

Since I was in Florida, I visited a friend named William. He was also a good friend of the Crouches. He invited Jan and I to dinner that night. As we all sat at the dinner table, I asked Jan how Paul was doing. She told me that Paul really liked me. I said I really cared about him. She told me that Paul needed a personal assistant and she asked me to consider taking the job.

Within two weeks, I was on my way to Southern California to start working with Paul Crouch. Here I was, actually working with the man who called me his "Key to the Middle East."

What I could never have expected was how God would use this relationship to open what would be a great door to reach Muslims around the whole world through one of the most effective mediums of Muslim evangelism in the world today - television.

CHAPTER 7

The Muslims

In each life, there are experiences God will use to accomplish His purposes.

Moses, who was educated in the ways of Egypt, confronted Pharaoh and brought about the deliverance of his people.

Daniel learned the ways of the Babylonians, and he became one of the highest ranking officials in Babylon and later Persia.

David learned on the shepherd's fields how to slay giants, protect sheep, and seek the heart of God.

From those powerful positions, each one glorified God and accomplished His purposes.

As I looked over my own life, I could also see a pattern. I was blessed to have been born and raised in the U.S., but I was originally from Jerusalem. Having lived in the Holy Land, I understood the language, culture and religion of my own people to where I knew how to communicate with them.

In the same city where the prophets and Jesus Himself ministered, I was visited by the Holy Spirit, and had my life radically changed. God seemed to be bringing all these puzzle pieces of my life together into a clear picture of my destiny.

Why did God choose me? Why did He reveal Himself to me so powerfully and then open so many doors for me in the ministry?

From the beginning of my relationship with God, I knew He wanted me to reach my own people: Palestinians, Arabs, and Muslims. They are the people I came from, and they were the nation from which God called me. He wanted me to love them, not to run away from them like I had previously been doing.

In Christ, I had found what my heart had always sought. He is the Living Water that quenches the thirst of the human soul. He is the Bread of Life Who satisfies the spiritual hunger in all our hearts.

The Muslims, like all people, are merely trying, in the ways they have been taught, to fill that hunger and satisfy that thirst. They are worshippers although they worship a different god. They have faith, although that faith is misdirected.

I know, because I was like them, and like them, I was seeking to please Allah by fulfilling, to the best of my ability, the five pillars of Islam.

But how will they know about the truth that can satisfy their spiritual thirst unless a preacher tells them? And how will a preacher tell them unless he is sent?

The burden in my heart grew as I realized how this awesome mission opportunity had barely been exploited. The more I learned, the greater the burden in my heart for these precious people.

There are around 1.2 billion Muslims in the world. Of these, around 300 million are Arabs from the 22 Arab countries in the Middle East and North

Africa.

Their story goes back to Ur of the Chaldees, and the call of the father of faith, Abraham. Around 4,000 years ago, God called the Patriarch to leave his home and go to the Promised Land. With his family, he went to Haran, in modern day Syria, where he stayed until his father died.

Afterwards, Abraham, his wife, and his nephew Lot continued their westward journey until they reached Shechem, modern day Nablus, in the northern Canaan. There, God reaffirmed His covenant that Abraham would be the one through whom a "seed" would come. Through that seed, all of the families of the earth would be blessed and restored into fellowship with God.

Abraham and his wife Sarah waited patiently for this promise to be fulfilled, but when Canaan was stricken with a severe famine, they grew weary and made a hasty, unnecessary trek into Egypt where there was food.

Abraham went to Egypt on his own initiative, and there, he fell into temptation. Frightened by Pharaoh's advances to Sarah, he lied. He said she was his sister rather than his wife. If not for God's intervention, Pharaoh would have ended up marrying Sarah, the prophet's wife. God brought down a slew of plagues against Pharaoh and his household.

Pharaoh called Abraham and reprimanded him for lying about the identity of his wife. As an act of penance, Pharaoh gave the aging prophet great gifts and sent him away from Egypt. One of those gifts was slaves.

Among them was a woman named Hagar who would rise through the ranks of the other slaves to the position of Sarah's personal hand maiden. They returned to the Holy Land, Canaan, as it was called, back to the place between Bethel and Ai where Abraham originally pitched his tent.

Years would pass, 12 to be exact, and there was no sign of a son, or seed, through whom God's great promises would be fulfilled. Sarah, in a depressed and yet magnanimous gesture, gives Abraham her handmaiden Hagar so he might have children with her. Abraham agrees.

He married Hagar, and she became pregnant. Hagar's pregnancy led to contention between Sarah and Hagar. When the handmaiden was found to be pregnant, she "despised" her mistress. Sarah abused Hagar who fled into the wilderness.

This is an important story because there are several extremely important "firsts" that occur in Hagar's trek in the wilderness. For one, she is met by an angel. But it is not just any angel. It is the Lord Jesus Christ Himself. This is the first Christophany, pre-incarnate appearance of Jesus Christ in the Bible. He tells Hagar that she will have a son she is to name "Ishmael." This is the first time God names a child in the scripture. His name means "God hears."

In obedience to the Lord, Hagar returns to Abraham and Sarah, and gives birth to the son. Ishmael was brought up as if he were the heir, the promised one. In fact, a few years later, when God commanded Abraham to circumcise all the males of his household as part of the new covenant, Ishmael was among those who were circumcised.

When Ishmael was around 13 years old, God came to Abraham and told him that Sarah would have a son. That son, Isaac, and NOT Ishmael, would be the one to whom the promise applied. He is the one through whom God's covenant with Abraham would be fulfilled.

After the birth of the new son, Isaac, the older son Ishmael grew envious. At the feast of Isaac's weaning, Ishmael mocked Isaac. Sarah then told Abraham to send Hagar and Ishmael away. God also told Abraham to do what Sarah said.

The next morning, Abraham complies. He gave Hagar a bottle of water and sent her and the boy into the desert. When the water ran out, Hagar threw her son under a bush, and went far enough away to not see the boy die. But then, Jesus comes again and opens her eyes. She then sees a well and draws water for the boy and herself. God promises her that 12 nations would come from her son and that he would be great.

There are many theories about Ishmael's relationship to the Arab people. Most believe that the Arabs are descended from Ishmael and those 12 nations he sired. Others say that the Arabs are also the descendents of Esau, as well as Lot's children, Moab and Ammon. Some also say that the Arabs are descended from Joktan, one of the descendents of Katurah, Abraham's wife after the death of Sarah. The truth is likely a combination of all of these.

Without delving too deeply into the genealogy of Ishmael and the others, we know there is a common belief among the Arabs that they are descended from Abraham through Ishmael. Islam is built on this belief. Although scripture is clear that Hagar and Ishmael were lost in the wilderness of Beersheba, which is located in southern Israel, Muslims believe she was lost in Arabia, and that the well that she found was the well of Zemzem, from which Muslims drink during their "hajj" pilgrimage.

In fact, it is the common belief among Muslims that God rejected Isaac's children, the Jews, and returned to Ishmael. This belief is further confirmed in the Islamic telling of the greatest story about Abraham in the Torah, the offering of Isaac at Mount Moriah. While the Bible specifically says that the son who was offered was Isaac, the Koran does not name the son. This omission in the Koran has been filled by the common belief among Muslims that it was Ishmael, and not Isaac, who was almost sacrificed on Mount Moriah. In fact, the Dome of the Rock in Jerusalem is believed to be the site of Abraham's sacrifice. Incidentally, the Jews also believe that the rock that is housed in the Dome of the Rock is the "Foundation Stone," the place where Abraham almost offered Isaac.

Here we have the root of Islam. It is based on the rejection of Ishmael, and a sense of injustice against this son. Islam seeks to rectify this injustice by elevating Ishmael, their perceived forefather, to the position of the preferred son.

It was in the deserts of Arabia that a young merchant named Mohammed would arise some 2,600 years after Abraham to claim the mantle of prophethood. He would find Biblical grounds for his new message, Islam, in his supposed blood relation to Ishmael.

He would marry a wealthy woman named Khadeeja who was several years his senior. He would run her business, and from her and her relatives, learn many of the beliefs of the Christians and the Jews. Some ancient texts indicate that she was a Christian, and that Mohammed married her in a Christian ceremony.

Be that as it may, Mohammed, who Muslims believe to have been illiterate, was something of a mystic. He would often go the caves to meditate and think about God. It was during one of these excursions that he claimed that the angel Gabriel came to him and told him to "recite," in Arabic "Iqra," three times.

From that time, Mohammed claimed to receive a series of revelations that were later compiled into the Koran. Each chapter of the Koran is called a "soura." There are 114 souras in the Koran which is equal in length to the New Testament.

One of Mohammed's stated goals was the restoration of monotheism. At the time, there was rampant paganism and worship of idols in the Arabian Peninsula. Mohammed even came to regard the Christian doctrine of the Trinity as a manifestation of this "polytheism." The Koran teaches that Christians believe in a trinity of gods: The Father, The Mother Mary and the Son Jesus. His mistaken view of the Trinity is revealed in Soura 5 (Table) verse

116: And (remember) when Allah will say (on the Day of Resurrection): "O 'Isa (Jesus), son of Maryam (Mary)! Did you say unto men: 'Worship me and my mother as two gods besides Allah?' "

This view of the trinity was taken from a heretical sect in Arabia.

Mohammed's message, as he saw it, would be the restoration of Abraham's monotheism. From the deserts of Arabia, Islam, by the power of the sword, grew rapidly. It spread to the entire peninsula, the Middle East, North Africa, and even made great gains into Christian Europe, nearly toppling Paris.

There are many aspects of Islam that can be traced to ancient customs and beliefs of Mohammed's day. There were elements of Zoroastrianism, Hinduism, Greek mythology and traditional Bedouin beliefs of the time in the Koran.

There is also an enormous amount of material from the Bible included in the Koran. There are great similarities between the Bible and the Koran, especially in relation to the Book of Genesis. The Koran teaches about Adam and Eve in the Garden of Eden, which the Koran says is in heaven. There is a story about Lucifer falling and becoming Satan, or "Al Shaytan."

While there are many similarities to the Bible, the stories in the Koran of the fall of man, and of Lucifer, do differ in significant ways from the Biblical versions.

There are also stories about Abraham, Ishmael, Joseph, Isaac, Jacob, David, Solomon, Jonah, Moses, Nimrod, Pharaoh, Noah and Enoch. Their names are changed in some cases, but the stories are remarkably similar, indicating that Mohammed had close contact with Jews and Christians who were in the Arabian Peninsula. One of his in-laws was Waraka bin Nawfal, a Christian priest, and cousin of Mohammed's first wife, Khadeeja. Waraka bin

Nawfal was a mystic who studied scripture extensively, and even had learned the original Hebrew language.

The Koran pays great homage to Moses who is mentioned 508 times. But, of particular interest to Christians, are Mohammed's teachings about Jesus.

In the Koran, Jesus is called "Isa." He is believed to be the son of the Virgin Mary. He is mentioned by name, Isa, 25 times; by title "Al Masih," 11 times, and as "Son of Mary," 23 times. There is a whole soura named after his mother "Mariam" which describes his birth. This is the only chapter in the Koran named after a woman.

There are many similarities between Isa of the Koran and Jesus of the Bible. First and foremost, Isa has the title of "Masih" in the Koran, which means Messiah. Secondly, Isa is born of a virgin named "Mariam." Isa also performs miracles, such as healing the blind, and raising the dead. Isa is rejected by the Jews, and is sentenced to death. He was taken up into heaven and will come again and judge the world.

But there are two points in the Koran which contradict the most central tenets of the Christian faith. Number one is the identity of the Messiah. The Koran, in several places proclaims that Isa is not the Son of God. The word used for son is "walad," which means "child," and is an important distinction with the word "Ibn," which means son. We will discuss this later.

There is a whole soura in the Koran that seeks to debunk Christ's Sonship. "Allah is one; He is unchanging. He is neither born, nor gives birth, and there is no one equal to him."

In this soura, which is very well known among Muslims, Islam states its belief that Jesus is not the Son of God, but there are other verses in the Koran that seem to dispute this.

There is also the issue of Christ's death. Muslims believe that Jesus did not die, but rather that God took Isa into heaven, and made one of His disciples to look like him. That other disciple was taken and crucified in His place.

This story is based on verse 157 of the Soura of the Women, "That they said (in boast), 'We killed Christ Jesus the son of Mary, the Messenger of Allah,'" but they killed him not, nor crucified him, but so it was made to appear to them, and those who differ therein are full of doubts, with no (certain) knowledge, but only conjecture to follow, for of a surety they killed him not."

There are other verses in the Koran that contradict this one, as well. This statement, when seen in context, doesn't say that He wasn't crucified or killed, but rather that it wasn't the Jews who crucified or killed Him. Be that as it may, the commonly held belief among Muslims is that He was taken into heaven, and a disciple, many believe, Judas Iscariot, was made to look like Isa and was crucified.

These two beliefs in Islam are the crux of the disagreement between Islam and Christianity. All of the other issues are peripheral compared to these central doctrines of the Christian faith.

In Mohammed's lifetime, Islam had spread to the whole Arabian Peninsula. Under the guidance of the Caliphs who followed Mohammed, Islam would spread eastward to Persia, Babylon, Baghdad, India and beyond. Westward, Islam had conquered much of Africa and was creeping northward into Europe but was stopped at the gates of Paris by Charlemagne. In southern Spain, the Moors had established themselves as a potent force.

When Palestine was conquered, and with it Jerusalem, the Vatican got involved, sending armies of Crusaders to battle for the Holy Land. These series of wars would forever strain the relationships between the Islamic East and the Christian West.

To this day, elements of this enmity persist. Most sadly, traces of this enmity are evident in the lack of missionary activity in the Arab and Muslim worlds. In the Seventies, some statistics show there was one known missionary for every one million Muslims. The number now offers some encouragement, but not much. There is now about one missionary for every 400,000 Muslims. It's been said, perhaps humorously, that there are more missionaries in the states of Alaska, with its 400,000 residents, than in the whole Muslim world.

In the meantime, God's Spirit is moving powerfully in the Muslim nations. There is a powerful, undeniable outpouring of the Holy Spirit on the Muslim and Arab worlds. According to statistics employed by Muslims clerics, and announced on the Al Jazeera News Station, there are six million Muslims in Africa coming to Jesus every year. That doesn't include the millions across Asia and the Middle East and the rest of the world.

A loud trumpet call has been sounded from heaven. God is calling His church to take up the responsibility to disciple these multitudes, many of whom risk their lives to follow the call of the Messiah.

Was God leading me to these people who I loved and longed to see experiencing the life I found in Christ? But, how? Every attempt I had made to reach out to my family was rebuffed. My father would have nothing to do with me.

There was the added dimension of my status as a "kaffir," or apostate, in the eyes of Muslims. The Koran says about those like me, "They but wish that ye should reject faith, as they do, and thus be on the same footing (as they): But take not friends from their ranks until they flee in the way of Allah (From what is forbidden). But if they turn renegades, seize them and slay them wherever ye find them."

Some Muslim scholars, especially those in the West, say this verse does not specifically deal with the ex-Muslims, but there are many other verses that lend credence to the death sentence for so-called apostates. In the largest Arab country, Egypt, it is called "hud el ridda." There are also many verses in the highly regarded commentaries of the Koran, including Sahih al Bukhari, supporting this judgment against ex-Muslims.

"...The Prophet said, 'If somebody (a Muslim) discards his religion, kill him.' " 52:260 Sahih Al Bukhari.

And, "Allah's Apostle never killed anyone except in one of the following three situations: (1) A person who killed somebody unjustly, was killed (in Qisas,) (2) a married person who committed illegal sexual intercourse and (3) a man who fought against Allah and His Apostle and deserted Islam and became an apostate." 83:37, Sahih Al Bukhari.

There are many other clear injunctions in the Koran and the commentaries on how to deal with people like me. In some cultures, so-called apostates are given three days to recant their apostasy, and return to Islam. If after those three days, they refuse, other means are implemented which could include: ostracism, threats, job loss; physical torture and, in many cases, death.

Often, these sentences are not carried out by the government, which might feign a human rights/freedom of religion policy, but rather the communities and families who carry out these injunctions.

For much of my early years as a Christian, I lived with fear of these commands. The paranoia I felt about being found out when I was in Florida was still haunting me. I always looked over my shoulder. I always felt the threat of Islam stalking me. Even in the safe environs of Hamilton, Alabama I found the fear nipping at my heels.

This same fear may also be one of the reasons why the church has been so lax about Muslim missions in the past. Horror stories about the way missionaries were mistreated created an impression of Islamic impenetrability. Although many put their hand to this plow and refused to look back, many either looked back, or never put their hands to the plow at all.

About the crucial question of how to reach Muslims, I appreciated the words of the Journal of Frontiers Missions. The book describes five ways that Jesus impacted His generation with the message of salvation:

Private words, prayers; planning with disciples to preach the Gospel

Visual words: His life, words and actions

Personal words: face to face evangelism with individuals including the Samaritan woman and Nicodemus

Proclaimed words: evangelism on a public scale like the Sermon on the Mount

Written words: including the Old Testament and later, the New Testament.

In his comments on these methods, David Barrett writes that today's Christians also have two new methods that were not available in Jesus' day: internet and television. In fact, several studies have shown that the most effective means of reaching Muslims is with television and the internet. They are personal and private, which avoids many of the dangers Muslims could face for wanting to study the Bible or learn about Jesus Christ.

Even though I was so young in my faith, I felt God leading me onto this very public platform from which to proclaim my faith, my conversion and my repudiation of Islam. Dr. Crouch, who had just started TBN's Arabic language Healing Channel, often encouraged me to host a program about my conversion to Christ. For three months, I rejected the idea as 'out of hand.' I didn't know what my family might do if they found out, and I still was, metaphorically, looking over my shoulder.

But after three months of Dr. Crouch's prodding, I understood that God was, indeed, calling me. I have found that one can pray for years that God use him or her.

There comes a day when God says, "O.K. I'm ready to use you."

At that point, a person who is sincere and willing must take the initiative and allow God to use him. When we pray that God send people into His harvest, we may actually be the answer to those prayers.

Chapter 8

Jesus

There is sometimes a divine sense of abandonment when a believer takes a leap out of his or her own circumstances, and is reminded of God's purposes for his or her own life, according to His Will.

To some degree, I had already taken some of these steps before. Some were dramatic. Some were costly. Some were uncertain. Some were occasioned by terrible misgivings and confusion. But, all together, those steps brought me here to this moment.

I was living in Southern California in constant contact with Paul Crouch, the founder of the world's biggest Christian television network, which had been a lifeline to me in my darkest hours.

Now, I was being asked to join them in an endeavor that matched my background, experience, calling and heart's cry: to host a program that would preach the Gospel in English and Arabic on stations that would carry the message to the unreached multitudes of the Middle East, Africa, Asia and the rest of the world.

While I was excited at the prospect, I knew this opportunity meant I had to face some of my greatest fears, and deal with them quickly and decisively. The number one fear is that which had plagued me since my early days back in the U.S. when I was a teenager in Florida: the eerily, discomfiting fear of being found out.

I was "out" already in a sense. My family knew about me, but there was still that sense of dread that lingered.

What if on some dark night, someone decided to carry out the Koran's dreaded command against ex-Muslims? "If they forsake you pursue them and kill them wherever you find them."

For an ex-Muslim, Jesus' words, "...there will come a day when those who kill you will think they are doing God service," are tangible and real. They are the mirror reflection of the Koran's oft-repeated admonitions of how to deal with infidels, and, more importantly, so-called, apostates.

The Koran's words were like an executioner with his sword, ready to strike at any moment. For many, the sword already fell. For others, the sword was on its final arc, falling to strike its intended victim.

Jesus' words, of course, were not just for ex-Muslims, but for all believers. "I have not come to bring peace, but a sword." But, for someone from a Muslim background, the words rang so familiar.

The difference between the sword of Islam and the sword of Christ is that Christ's sword is not used to win converts. In fact, it is not even to be found in the hands of His followers. Rather, it is the swords of those who refuse to accept Christ, and it is used against those who try to win them to Christ.

In the freedom of the United States and most of the Western world, this sword has been sheathed in the language of human rights and civil protections. But in the East, this sword is easily and regularly unsheathed. It strikes quickly, mercilessly.

It is a sword that strikes once every five minutes around the world, according to a report in the "Church of England Newspaper." That's 12 times per hour, 288 times per day, and 105,000 times per year.

Once every five minutes is a conservative estimate. Some say the number of Christian martyrs around the world is closer to 160,000 per year. That would mean the sword falls once every three minutes.

When you're an ex-Muslim, those words, "…those who kill you will think they are doing God's service," quickly jump out of the pages of the Gospel of John with an eerie familiarity. We heard those exact words before, only from the other side of that sword.

Jesus predicted them.

At first, the words agitate. Then they frustrate. Then, if you allow yourself, you wrestle with them like Jacob wrestled with God alone at night. But, when the first rays of sunshine broke through the night chill, the Divine Wrestler wanted to go back to heaven, but Jacob wouldn't let Him leave until He granted him a blessing.

For the believer who engages in this wrestling match, the blessing is this divine sense of abandonment, "My life belongs to Him, and it is His to use as He sees fit. I have no claim on my life for it is His. I've been bought and paid for by the blood of the Lamb. And if, like Him, I am called to lay down my life, I am ready. For to live is Christ, and to die is gain."

At first, Jesus' warning feels like a cold winter chill that makes us shiver, but when we embrace those words, they become a powerful gale that fills our sails and propels us forward.

I accepted Dr. Crouch's offer to begin the program. The experience reminded me of the first time I spoke in public at the reconciliation conference back in Alabama. Someone just put a microphone in my hand and told me to, "Talk."

What would I say?

I felt so small on that stage, and I felt so small before this new challenge.

What should I say? What is my message? How should it be presented?

Arabic Christian television stations had increased dramatically in the past decade. There were several satellite Christian stations broadcasting into areas that had been previously impenetrable to the Gospel. The work was proceeding at break-neck speed.

I watched many of the programs that were being broadcast to the Muslim world in Arabic and English. A huge focus of these programs was the disproving of the Koran. Many of the hosts were ex-Muslims, like me. They were reared in Islam, but were touched by Christ, and were now sharing their conversion testimonies on television.

The stories were awesome and awe-inspiring. The impact was enormous, as Muslims around the world were writing in to say they had accepted Christ, to ask questions, to ask for materials and Bibles. The global impact of Arabic Christian television was enormous.

As one who had lived on both sides of the East-West cultural divide, I felt I could use my background to fulfill the Biblical mandate as prescribed in Titus 2:10, "...make the Gospel of God attractive."

At first, I thought to make my program about Islamics: the study of Islam, and using resources of Islam, to expose its contradictions and inconsistencies. Islamics have been an effective tool used in much of Christian programming to win Muslims.

But, as I thought about using this method, I felt uneasy.

Did I want to make this pulpit God was giving me into a launching pad from which to attack Islam?

As I wrestled with this question, I spoke with Dr. Crouch's personal physician Dr. Raafat Girgis. A great believer, he spoke to me words that really touched my life.

He said, "Hazem, you love Jesus more than you hate Islam."

He was right.

I didn't just want to berate Islam. Muslims, who may watch my show, already know Islam. Most have lived their whole lives under its dictates and cultural sway. Like me, they know the darkness and emptiness that is there.

Why should I focus more attention on that darkness?

A man groping in darkness doesn't need a lesson on darkness; he needs light. That light is Jesus.

As John 1 says, "In Him was life, and that life is the light of man."

Dr. Girgis' words gave me a new strategy. Part of that strategy lay in the name of the program, with which Dr. Girgis also helped me: Reflections.

In Arabic, the program is called Khawater Aber, which means the reflections of an ex-Muslim. In English it was shortened to just Reflections.

In each program, I discuss some of the lessons I learned on my way out of Islam into the Kingdom of God. I also describe some of the struggles I had as I came to grips with God's call and destiny in my life.

As I was pondering my next steps in relation to the program, Dr. Crouch asked me to join him on his daily live program on TBN called Behind the Scenes. Dr. Crouch introduced and described my program, his vision for it, and its goals. I sat by on the dais, not sure what to expect. But during the program, several viewers called in to pledge financial support for the program. We raised enough money to start filming.

The only question left unanswered was what would I say?

I knew that I didn't want to focus on Islam incessantly. I knew I didn't want to make it like so many other Christian programs: a man sitting behind a desk talking and answering phone calls. In my spirit, I had an impression of what I wanted to accomplish with the program. I wanted to use words and images, colors and music in a unique fashion to where people would watch because they were drawn.

After much prayer and meditation, I knew what my first program would be about. My subject was the One around whom my whole life revolved. The One who changed my life, and the only One Who could change the lives of my viewers: Jesus.

No one in human history has impacted the world like He has.

In Arabic for the Healing Channel, and in English for the JCTV (TBN's youth channel), I would attempt to describe who Jesus was to me.

The more I delved into my subject, the more I realized what an enormous feat laid before me. Jesus is the central figure of human history. Time itself is divided into the period before His birth and after His death.

He changed the world in more ways than I could begin to expound in a half hour program. The whole known world was turned upside down by His followers who pledged life and blood to follow in His steps.

What could I offer? What words could I use to bring glory to the One whose glory fills all the heavens and the earth? What beauty could I employ to describe the One whose life had been depicted everywhere from Megiddo and the Catacombs of Rome to the Vatican and the Guggenheim Museum in New York City. His life of three decades had been recounted by history's greatest artists from Leonardo Da Vinci to Franco Zeffarelli; from Pablo Picasso to Mel Gibson; from Caravaggio to Thomas Kinkade.

With a subject as great as the Son of God, it was easy to be overwhelmed by the awesomeness of the responsibility of presenting Him in an attractive way. After much thought and prayer, I understood what I had that no one else had – my testimony.

The Bible says, "...they overcame the devil by the word of their testimony."

This is one of the most powerful tools we have as believers to proclaim His gospel.

The program had to be about my experience with Jesus. That experience would bring in elements of my Islamic upbringing and education. It would include the words I had heard from Christians. It would also include the solid foundation I found myself standing on, based on my personal experiences, with the Son of God, the Creator of the Universe.

Since my target audience was Muslims, the program would have to include what I believed as a Muslim. I started writing, and the words flowed out so easily. I knew that God was anointing me.

This first program would be called, Who is Jesus? It turned into a treatise not just about Who Jesus is, but Who He is not. So much of the Bible deals with these two issues and, in our hearts; we all have to deal with this question: Who is Jesus?

Because Islam was spread by the sword, I felt I should address this issue of bloodshed. There is a huge difference between what Jesus taught about bloodshed and what Mohammed taught about it. It wasn't our enemy's blood that had to be shed; it was Jesus' own blood that was shed.

In this episode, I never mentioned the name Mohammed which brings no light. It was all about Jesus. The music, the artwork and the sermon all pointed to Him.

The episode has been broadcast countless times on television stations around the world, sharing the message of the God who changed my life.

WHO IS JESUS

I found Jesus Christ was the Prince of Peace, not war. I learned of how Christ spread his message with compassion and not by gruesome bloody wars. His disciples were martyred for their faith, never using violence to advance their cause. Christ forgave and converted murderers and thieves. He forgave sinful adulterers. Christ gave life and didn't kill one soul, teaching us that those who live by the sword, also die by the sword.

Instead of preaching dead ritual, Christ preached faith in God's love and His ability to have mercy upon us. Instead of shedding blood, Christ shed his blood for the sake of a fallen humanity. Instead of cursing people, Christ forgave and loved them. Instead of adopting man made strategies like war and hate, upon his enemies, Christ taught us to love everyone... even our enemies. Instead of trying to grow his kingdom here on earth, Jesus said that his kingdom is not of this world. Instead of being selective and denying certain people love, Christ instructed us to preach the gospel to every creature. Instead of conquering lands and peoples, Christ conquered Satan, and sins grasp upon humanity was broken. I found out about his tomb and how, to this day, it is empty, and how his body is still nowhere to be found.

It was a revelation that Jesus is the only worthy person fit to be a King of kings. Because He is the King, the King of heaven, the King of glory, and the King of ages. He is the Lord of lords…

I mean, wouldn't you desire to know such a great king?

The angel said, "Do not be afraid, Mary, you have found favor with God. You will be with child and give birth to a son, and you are to give him the name Jesus. He will be great, and will be called the Son of the Most High."

John the Baptist said of him, "Behold, the Lamb of God which does take away the sins of the world."

Peter, when asked, made a bold declaration!

Jesus asked him, "Who do YOU, Peter, say that I am?

Peter responded, saying, "Thou art the Christos, Son of the living God."

The Roman centurion said of this crucified, miracle working Jesus, "Surely, this IS the Son of God."

This is who Jesus is!

He is the Son of God. No boundaries are able to measure his infinite love. His love is powerful! It contains no barrier and has no limits; it's immeasurable. His mercies! His mercies are new every morning. His leadership is perfect. He's a good King. He saves sinners from sin. He heals the sick. He feeds the hungry. He quenches the thirsty. He encourages the discouraged. He cleanses the lepers. He restores sight to the blind, and He sets the captives free.

He is all-sufficient. He is all mighty. He is all knowing. He is all-powerful.

He is all seeing and all hearing. He is the truest philosophy. He is the very core of true theology. He is the greatest miracle in all history. In fact, he split history with his birth: BC to AD. Before Christ to "The Year of Our Lord."

This is Jesus: my great King.

If there is a need, He supplies it. If there is a wound, He cures it. If there is doubt, He destroys it. If you are weak, He will strengthen you. If you are tempted, He delivers you. If you are tested, He helps you. If you have pain, He relates to you. If you are lonely, He will be with you. If you are broken, He will mend you. If you're a sinner, He will save you. If you are lost, He will find you.

This is who my Jesus is.

If you are small, He is big. If you are big, He is bigger. If you are humble, He will exalt you. If you are proud, He will humble you. If you are young, He will watch you. If you are old, He will assist you. If you are diligent, He will reward you. And if you weep, He will weep with you. If you laugh, He will laugh with you. He was in the beginning, and before that, He was. And for all eternity, He will be.

Have you ever met this Jesus before?

If you are poor in spirit, his kingdom He gives you. If you mourn, comfort He offers you. If you are meek, inheritance He leaves you. If you hunger and thirst for righteousness, He will fill you. If you're merciful, mercy He gives to you. If you're pure in heart, His face he shows you. If you're a peacemaker, His son he names you. If people betrayed you, if they deny you or doubt you, He will walk with you because Judas betrayed him, the religious leaders denied him, and Thomas doubted Him. The Jews didn't want Him. The Romans; they crucified Him. In the tomb, they laid Him. But He refused to stay. On the third day, He was ...resurrected. Men laid Him in the tomb, but God seated Him on the throne. This is who Jesus is.

He will give you love, joy, peace, patience, kindness, goodness, meekness, faithfulness and self-control. Why? Because He IS all of these things. He is love, joy, peace, patience, kindness, goodness, meekness, faithfulness. For He made known to man, the path of life. In his presence, there is fullness of joy, and at his right hand, there are pleasures forevermore.

This is who Jesus is to the Christian. Don't you want to know such a God?

He is the key to peace. He is the well of wisdom. He is the door to the Father. He is the gateway to heaven. His promises are true. His love is endless. His face is glorious. His light is overwhelming. His yoke is easy. His burden is light. He is… irresistible.

Angels bow to Him. Sinners need Him. Christians worship Him. Presidents admire Him. Kings don't understand Him. Historians can't erase Him. Scientists can't disqualify Him. Atheists can't ignore Him. Satan fears Him. Mountains melt like wax before Him. The roaring seas obey Him, and the crashing waves, well… He walks on them. Children are attracted to Him because He is the bread of heaven, and he is the water of life. He is the Lilly in your valley, and He is the Rose on your mountaintop. He is the Lord of Lords and the King of all kings. .

This is who Jesus is to us Christians. Don't you want to know such a God?

All the authors of the Earth can't write enough about Him. All the paper on the earth can't hold everything written about Him. All the ink in this world wouldn't be enough to explain Him. His words are forever established. His throne is forever immovable. His kingdom is forever eternal.

This is my Lord.

He loves patiently. He loves gently. He does not envy. He does not boast. He is not proud. He is not rude. He is not self-seeking. He is not easily angered. He keeps no record of wrongs for us who know him. He does not delight in evil. He rejoices with the truth. He always protects. He's always trustworthy. He never, ever fails. His love is indescribable, and His grace is always sufficient.

This is my God.

He is a good God. He is a good Father. He is a good Savior. In Him, we live, in Him we move, in Him, we have our being. There is no religious leader like him. There was never anyone close to being like Him, and never will there be anyone to the likes of Him. He didn't appoint any successors: He only appointed sons and called upon friends. He is the Alpha and the Omega. He is the beginning and the end. He is omnipotent. He is omniscient. He is omnipresent. He is the only one who has loved us and loosed us from our sins by His blood. He alone is worthy of our worship. He is the great Lion and the gentle Lamb. He is the humble servant and the victorious King who triumphs over all. The Earth is the Lord's and the fullness thereof. For His is the kingdom; and His is the power; and his is the glory, forever and ever. Amen.

He turned water into wine. With a little boy's lunch, He fed the five thousand. He turned darkness into light. He turned disease into health, and He brought the dead back to life; for He is the resurrection and the life. He is the mediator between God and Man. He is the only worthy High Priest. He is the image of the invisible God. He is Prince of peace. He is the light of the world. He swallowed up death forever and brought shame to shame itself. I love Him because He... He first loved me.

This is Jesus. He is Lord! The Lord of heaven and the Lord of glory. The Lord of the church, and He is... my... Lord. The Lord, our Shepherd; The Lord our Provider; The Lord our Peace; The Lord our Healer; The Lord our righteousness; The Lord: This is Jesus. He is Lord! The Lord of heaven and the Lord of Glory. The Lord of the church; and He is… my lord. The Lord our Shepherd; The Lord our Provider; The Lord our Peace; The Lord our Healer; The Lord our righteousness; The Lord who hears; The Lord our Banner; The Lord who Sanctifies; Soon to be Lord over all the earth. Soon to be YOUR Lord.

Do you want to know him?

He is fairest of ten thousand men, dressed in a robe reaching down to his feet, and has a golden sash around His chest. His head and hair are white like wool, as white as snow, and His eyes are like… like a blazing… fire. His feet are like bronze, glowing in a furnace, and His voice is like the sound of rushing waters. In His right hand, He holds seven stars, and out of His mouth comes a sharp, double-edged sword. His face is brighter than the noon day sun shining --- in all its brilliance, for He shines brighter than the brightest star in the hearts of us who believe. In fact, he is the bright and morning star.

This is who Jesus is. Don't you want to know such a Saviour?

I learned from the wrestling and toil that went into this first episode, how to hear the guidance of the Holy Spirit in producing future programs. My next episode was about books in a library. So much of the controversy in my life had been about books, two books: the Bible and the Koran.

The next episode was called The Beach. On the sunny, southern California coast, I spoke about the innumerable grains of sand. In the book of Psalms, David said that God's thoughts toward us are more numerous than the grains of sand.

I wanted through this program to show how this God, Jehovah, was not like Allah of Islam. He was not distant and untouchable. He was close. He was so close to each of us that He couldn't stop thinking about us. He couldn't stop watching us and thinking about all of our ways.

Then the subject matters of my episodes started flowing out: light, prison, names, identity, and the prodigal son. When the first season was complete, I had finished 13 episodes in English and 13 in Arabic. They were being broadcast all over the world.

In time, the program grew from its original airing on the Healing Channel and JCTV to also being aired on several other stations including: Church Channel, TBN, Al Karma and Al Fady.

The program quickly reached the top 10 of all programs aired on the Church Channel. It was number seven, to be exact. It was overwhelming to think of all the people whose lives God was allowing me to reach through this great pulpit.

I was especially blessed to hear how God was using the program to reach Muslims. One woman wrote to me and said that she had been plagued by nightmares. Awakened one night by the nightmares, she turned on her television, and saw me speaking in Arabic. She said the words ministered to her heart. She fell back asleep and had a dream about Jesus coming to her. She gave her life to the Lord, as a result.

With the completion of the first season, Dr. Crouch encouraged me to start working on the second season. In addition to the specific subject matters, I also interviewed some of the great preachers of our time including Benny Hinn; Arthur Blessit, who had walked around the world carrying a cross, and Bill Wiese who wrote the best seller 23 Minutes in Hell.

I also interviewed other Muslim background believers who shared their own miraculous journeys out of Islam, including Yohanna Zakaria and Steve (Husein), the one who prayed the sinner's prayer with me.

I also set up a website for the program with my testimony and episodes of the programs that had already aired. I was blown away by the way God was using the programs.

CHAPTER 9

The Railroad

Some of the episodes of Reflections mirrored my own life and the struggles I was going through. Few times was this as evident as with the episode called The Railroad.

For that episode, I stood or walked next to a railroad and described the fleeting nature of our lives. I spoke about the reasons for our existence. I also discussed how our lives are sometimes hit with unexpected events, like the tsunami that had hit Indonesia, claiming so many lives there.

As I spoke those words, there was a tsunami of events swirling around me. They were related to my family. This made it easy to conjure up the emotions I wanted to convey through this episode because I was actually walking down that track in real life.

The loss of family relationships are one of the crosses we all have to bear. Jesus said, "If any man loves mother or father more than me, he is not worthy of me."

When Jesus called disciples in Matthew 8, one man said he wanted to first go bury his father.

Jesus told him, "Let the dead bury their dead, you follow Me."

There are many other crosses we bear in our lives, including self-love, the love of riches, and the lusts of the flesh. These are all things that arise within our hearts and bid for first place in our hearts before Jesus Christ.

For an ex-Muslim, the loss of family relationships is often the hardest cross to bear. There are so many conflicted emotions we feel towards our families: love, loyalty, guilt, anger. The Bible is clear in its teaching that we are to love and honor our parents and relatives. We need to be careful, however, because that love and commitment could easily become a hindrance if it interferes with our love and service to God.

This issue came to a head for me in 2010. The show was doing very well. I felt my ministry was effective, and more importantly, I was growing in my relationship with God and with others.

I had already seen the impact of the program through the many lives that were being touched and changed. On my website, I received scores of comments of viewers who said they appreciated and were touched by the program, but in my heart, I was conflicted.

I was so honored to be used by God in this way, and yet I had this deep longing and sense of responsibility to see my own family come into God's kingdom and be liberated from the shackles of Islam. How could I be rejoicing in His love and glory while my family was still groping in the darkness?

There is a natural love we all have for our families. It is the natural love that all people share. Solomon in the Book of Proverbs says, "Above all things, guard your heart, for out of it, proceeds the issues of life." The word "heart" in some translations is "affections."

"Guard your affections." Be careful what you allow yourself to fall in love with. The things we love can rule us, and if we don't rule our affections, they can destroy us.

Like all things from our un-regenerated natures, this natural, soulical love of family must pass through Calvary so that it, too, is brought into submission to the Holy Spirit. At Calvary, it can die to its selfish elements so it can be raised to a spiritual love. For me, this was one of the most painful times I passed through.

In his book Pursuing God, A.W. Tozer describes this deliverance from the tyranny of the flesh, "Let us remember, when we talk of the rending of the veil, we are speaking in a figure, and the thought of it is poetical, almost pleasant; but in actuality, there is nothing pleasant about it. In human experience, that veil is made of living spiritual tissue; it is composed of the sentient, quivering stuff of which our whole beings consist, and to touch it is to touch us where we feel pain. To tear it away is to injure us, to hurt us and make us bleed. To say otherwise is to make the cross no cross and death no death at all. It is never fun to die. To rip through the dear and tender stuff of which life is made can never be anything but deeply painful. Yet that is what the cross did to Jesus and it is what the cross would do to every man to set him free."

I wanted to know how to love my family and, if possible, to be reconciled to them, but at the same time, I knew what the consequences of my continued work on television would mean.

Soon after the program Reflections began airing on the Arabic language, Healing Channel, my family got wind of it. I held no fantasy about what would happen once my family knew. I knew their reaction would be painful.

In many ways, I still felt like that 17-year-old boy who left home to attend college and ended up breaking away from my family's control. One of the consequences of that choice was that I now had no physical family to support me. I was still single, and my only family was the family of Christ.

Believers had always been family to me from the Mobaraks in Birmingham to the Bajalias in Maylene and the Saylors in Winfield. God had been so faithful to His promise that I would "... receive 100-fold in this life."

But every now and then, pangs of loneliness seem to spring up out of nowhere. They would slam into my heart like waves against a rock. I knew the verses and understood my unique situation, and yet, still, those pangs still hurt. We long for those siblings and relatives we were raised with. We long for the smells of home, the camaraderie, and unique relationships we find among our relatives.

I was also very aware of how much pain and shame I had already caused them. So much of the Middle Eastern family structure is built around the clan and the community. Our whole worlds revolve around each other.

On the one hand, this is a wonderful source of warmth and community that outsiders look at with envy. Along with the deep sense of community, is a shared sense of responsibility and care for one another, but it's a double edged sword. If you're on the inside, the benefits and camaraderie can be deep and meaningful, but it's a completely different story once this "community" is turned against you. It can be vicious, and it was for my family.

The greatest shame for any Muslim family is for their child to turn from Islam, and become, as I had, in their eyes, an apostate. To be an apostate is the highest form of treason and betrayal to a family.

There is some disagreement within Islam about the actual meaning of the Koranic verses that call for the execution of apostates, but within the families and communities there are no such questions. It is clear what will be done to apostates.

To my family, I was an apostate. Not only that; I was now preaching the religion that was so despised, Christianity. In addition, I was trying to get Muslims to leave Islam for Christianity, and I was doing it from multiple international platforms in Arabic and English.

Having been raised in this culture, I was so aware of the shame that my father was experiencing because of me. I had no doubts or regrets about what I was doing on television or why I was doing it. I had no reservations. I knew I had to preach the Gospel, no matter what, but I also had to come to grips with what was being done to my family because of it.

Shortly after the program Reflections began airing, some of my siblings contacted me. They said my father, who was back in Palestine, was suffering greatly in the community because of me. His brothers mocked him and blamed him for my apostasy. Others blamed my mother, and some, my step mother.

My older brother Waleed asked three different Imams what should be done with me. Two of them told him I was to be killed. Another said that the family should try to love me back into Islam. They were to woo me back with compassion and kindness.

At the time, I was studying Christian theology through a correspondence course that was based in Florida. Having finished my bachelor's degree, I went down to Florida for the graduation ceremony. While in Florida, I spent a week with my family.

It was a stunning contrast with what happened the last time I saw them in 2004. Their kindness and sincerity was so compelling. I wanted so much for my family to be this way, so wholesome.

Waleed, who had assumed the role of family leader since my dad was in the Middle East, wanted me to come back to Florida and be restored to the family. He said I could go back to school and start all over again. It was a wonderful time of getting to know my family again and meeting some of their children for the first time.

After I left Florida, Waleed called me several times and he suggested ways that we could start over. One of the key elements of this new beginning would be that he and I would enroll in a special Islamic Theological Center where I could really learn the truth about Islam that he felt had eluded me.

My faith in Christ was strong. I had no illusions about discovering some secret in Islam that would win me back. I didn't want to study Islam to see if I had missed something. Rather, I saw that my family was now engaging me in the conversation that I really wanted to have with them. If studying Islam with him would open the way for me to prove to them that the gospel is true, I was willing to do it.

Around January 2010, I told Waleed that I was willing to study Islam with him. For me, it would be like a comparative religion course. I would learn what they taught but I would also explain to them the faults I found in Islam which I hoped would get them to accept Christ as well. The classes were to begin in July that summer.

A struggle ensued in my heart as I weighed these thoughts. My family seemed so sincere in their desire to reconcile with me and to take me back as one of them. But with time, their true intentions started to show. For one, Waleed told me that I had to come to the classes to learn Islam and not to compare it to Christianity or to find faults in it. I told my brother that I couldn't just disregard all the holes that I knew about in Islam.

As the time for the classes drew closer, his preconditions increased. I started to realize that this was not a viable option.

What really closed the door for me was a final precondition that came from my father back in Palestine. To be welcomed back into the family, my father said I had to go on Islamic television and say that I was simply not in my right mind when I made the television programs on TBN. I would have to renounce Christianity and embrace Islam on international Islamic TV.

I would never renounce Christ. I would never deny His love. As much as I loved my family and longed to be reconciled to them, it could not happen on their terms. The struggle in my heart subsided some as I realized that I had to continue, unhindered, on the path that God had placed before me.

The confrontation with my family drove me to find out exactly why I was a Christian and why I wasn't a Muslim.

CHAPTER 10

Why I'm not a Muslim

Whenever dealing with the subject of Islam, I always like to differentiate between Muslims and Islam. Muslims are the people who adhere to Islam. Islam is the religion itself. Anyone who knows Muslims knows that there is often a genuine sincerity and goodness about them. The vast majority of Muslims are gracious people who want so much to please God. They are completely unlike what we usually see in the media.

The problem is not with Muslims. It is with Islam, the actual religion. There are many aspects of Islam that I could never accept. My first problem is with founder of Islam himself, Mohamed. His lifestyle begs for a sincere evaluation of whether he was a holy man or not.

Mohammed

Born in Mecca around 570 A.D., Mohammed claimed to have had visitations by the Angel Gabriel who supposedly gave him passages of the Koran which were recited from the immutable Preserved Tablets in heaven.

During the early years of his calling as a messenger, Mohammed preached his new religion as a monotheistic alternative to the idol worship that was prominent in Arabia. He was met with great resistance in Mecca and eventually fled north to Medina. There, his message was embraced, and he gained a large band of followers, numbering as many as 10,000. With these armies, he returned to Mecca, which he conquered along with much of the Arabia, which he considered the Islamic Caliphate.

Mohammed had many encounters with the Christians and Jews of his day. Many of the stories in the Koran are corruptions of the Biblical stories about Moses, Joseph, Pharaoh, Isaac, Abraham, Ishmael, Hagar, Sarah, Edris (Enoch) and even Jesus (Isa).

There are many aspects of the life of Mohammed that I see as inconsistent with the character of a man of God. For one: his wives. He had 13 wives, not counting his concubines and slave girls. Although his first wife, Khadeja, died before he did, at least 11 of his wives outlived him. He died when he was 63 years old.

The common belief is that Mohammed had 11 of these wives at one time. The most disturbing of these unions was that with Aisha, the daughter of his friend Abu Bakr. He betrothed her at the tender age of six and consummated the marriage when she was nine years old. He was 56 at the time.

Some will compare Mohammed sexual dalliances with King Solomon in the Old Testament, of whom it says, he had 300 wives and nearly 600 concubines. But one need only read to the end of Solomon's life story to see what is said about the effect of his sexual exploits: As Solomon grew old, his wives turned his heart after other gods, and his heart was not fully devoted to the LORD his God, as the heart of David his father had been.

King Solomon died an idolater for his lifestyle. There is a serious warning that his lifestyle was dangerous and an example not to be followed. But in Mohammed's case, his marriages were seen as a virtue. They are justified and his lifestyle is seen and exemplary. The child brides and polygamy in the Muslim world show that Mohammed is held up as an example to emulate.

Another marriage that is particularly embarrassing is that of Mohammed and Zaynab. This woman was a cousin of Mohammed who had originally married his adopted son Zayd.

Mohammed asked that Zayd divorce her so he could marry her. To justify this union, which was forbidden by Islam, Mohammed said he obtained divine sanction in a new Koranic verse in which God commands Mohammed to follow his desire and marry Zaynab.

Although Mohammed claimed to have the sexual prowess of 30 men, he also had a great disregard for women as reflected in the Sahih Al Bokhary (one of most respected commentaries on the Koran). It says, "The Messenger of Allah (peace and blessings of Allah be upon him) said, 'I was shown Hell and I have never seen anything more terrifying than it. And I saw that the majority of its people are women.'"

They said, "Why, O Messenger of Allah?"

He said, "Because of their ingratitude."

It was said, "Are they ungrateful to Allah?"

He said, "They are ungrateful to their companions (husbands) and ungrateful for good treatment. If you are kind to one of them for a lifetime then she sees one (undesirable) thing in you, she will say, 'I have never had anything good from you.'" (Narrated by al-Bukhaari, 1052).

The strictly patriarchal family system of Arabia was enshrined in the Koran even to the point of advocating violence against wives as described in this verse 4:34, "Virtuous women are obedient, careful, during the husband's absence, because God has, of them, been careful. But chide those for whose refractoriness you have cause to fear; remove them into beds apart, and scourge them: but if they are obedient to you, then seek not occasion against them: verily, God is High, Great!"

This same passage says that women are not only to be beaten if a husband is suspicious, but it also says that women are blatantly inferior to men by nature, "Men are superior to women on account of the qualities with which God has gifted the one above the other, and on account of the outlay they make from their substance for them."

Some Muslims argue that the injunctions against women are primarily in the commentaries which are not regarded as the word of God. But these verses are not from some commentary, or fatwa, but the Koran itself.

In the Sahih Al Bukhari 1:6: 301, Mohammed was asked about why women's intelligence is deficient, "O Allah's Apostle! What is deficient in our intelligence and religion?"

He said, "Is not the evidence of two women equal to the witness of one man?"

They replied in the affirmative.

He said, "This is the deficiency in her intelligence. Isn't it true that a woman can neither pray nor fast during her menses (menstrual cycle)?"

The women replied in the affirmative.

He said, "This is the deficiency in her religion."

There are many other aspects of Mohammed's life and teachings that I could not accept. Islam is a religion of violence that encourages the maiming and murder of those who refuse to accept it. I was shocked to learn of the way Mohammed approved of the death of Asmaa bint Marwan while she was breastfeeding her child.

According to several Islamic sources, including hadiths, Asmaa was a poet from the city of Medina who opposed Mohammed. When he got wind of it, Mohammed said, "Who will rid me of the daughter of Marwan?"

A blind man supposedly entered her home at night while she was asleep, with her five children around her, including one suckling who was at her breast. The man took the baby away, and stabbed Asmaa in her heart.

When he was told of what his follower did, Mohammed responded, "No two goats will lock horns over her."

There is another story of Um Qirfa. This incident occurred about six years after Mohammed moved to Medina. There was a pagan tribe called Banu Fazara. When they were set upon by Mohammed and his warriors, they concocted a plan to kill Mohammed, but Mohammed's armies overpowered them. A mother of Um Qirfa and her daughter escaped, but were captured.

After their capture, the mother was handed to Mohammed's follower "Qais," who took the old woman and tied her limbs to camels that were then whipped so that they would walk in opposite directions tearing her apart limb by limb. The daughter, who was very beautiful, was sold into slavery.

But it wasn't just these tales of horror that drove me away from Islam. There are many more.

The Koran

The Koran is also filled with historical, geographical and scientific errors. One of the well known historical errors of the Koran is the issue of Mary, the mother of Jesus, who is known as "Miryam." While she is held in great honor, the Koran frequently mistakes "Miryam," the mother of Jesus, for "Miryam" the sister of Moses.

In Arabic, the names of Jesus' mother and the Moses' sister are the same: Miryam. Mohammed apparently heard of the two women and mistook them for each other. There are at least three places in the Koran where this mistake is made.

In Soura 3, the mother of Moses and Aaron, says of her daughter Miryam, "Lord, I have vowed to Thee, in dedication, what is within my womb. Receive Thou this from me; Thou hearest, and knowest.' And when she gave birth to her she said, 'Lord, I have given birth to her, a female.' (And God knew very well what she had given birth to; the male is not as the female.) 'And I have named her Miryam, and commend her to Thee with her seed, to protect them from the accursed Satan.'"

Later in the chapter it says, "O Miryam! Allah giveth thee glad tidings of a Word from Him: his name will be Christ Jesus, the son of Miryam, held in honour in this world and the Hereafter."

This Soura is called Imran, which is a reference to the father of Moses, Aaron and Miryam, so it is clear that Mohammed simply mistook the two Miryams.

Soura 19:27-28, says, "O Mary! Truly a strange thing has thou brought! O sister of Aaron, thy father was not a man of evil, nor your mother a woman unchaste!"

This verse again is directed at Mary the mother of Jesus, and yet she is called "Sister of Aaron." Indeed, the Torah says there is a Miryam who is the sister of Aaron, but she is not the mother of Jesus, except in the Koran.

This error is repeated in Soura 66:12, where Mary, the mother of Jesus, is called the daughter of Imran. Again, there is a "Miryam" who is the daughter of Imran. She is also the sister of Aaron, and she is also the daughter of Imran's wife, but she is not the mother of Jesus. There are 1,500 years between the two, a glaring historical error in the Koran repeated several times.

There are many other historical errors in the Koran as well. Alexander the Great, who is called the "two-horned one," is said to have been a monotheist who lived to a ripe old age. Both of these were false. He spread the Greek religion and philosophy that was the most prominent form of polytheism in the known world. He died at the age of 30.

In Soura 28, the Koran describes Pharaoh commanding his minister Haman to build a tower to heaven so he could see Moses' God. There are several historical errors in this account. First of all, Haman lived almost 1,000 years after the pharaoh who was concerned with Moses. Secondly, Haman lived in Persia, more than 1,200 miles away from Egypt. We could also point out that the tower was built in Babylon, modern day Iraq. But the Koran says that the tower was built by Egyptians using sun-baked bricks.

Looking at this verse from a historical point of view, the Tower of Babel was built around 2,000 years before Christ. Pharaoh and Moses lived around 1,350 before Christ. Haman lived around 470 B.C. Between Haman and the Tower are about 1,300 years. Between Haman and Pharaoh are almost 1,000 years. The Koran lumps all of these stories together into one time period.

In Soura 20, the Koran says that the Samaritans deceived the Israelites into making the golden calf and were reprimanded by Moses. Again this is historically inaccurate. The golden calf was made by the Israelites around 1,300 B.C., soon after they left Egypt and started wandering in the Sinai.

The Bible goes into great length to describe the time, and the way, the Samaritans came into existence. It was after the Northern Kingdom Israel was taken into captivity by the King of Assyria, around 740 B.C. There were almost six centuries (600 years) between the Samaritans and the golden calf, but the Koran, again, erroneously lumps them together.

The scientific errors in the Koran are numerous as well. Among the most glaring is the verse that says that the human fetus is formed, bones first, then the flesh wraps around the bones. In addition to this scientifically inaccurate picture of the formation of the fetus, the Koran says that semen is formed between the spine and the ribs, "Now let man but think from what he is created! He is created from a drop emitted – proceeding from between the back bone and the ribs." 86:5-7.

According the Islamic teaching, the Koran is the exact words of Allah, taken from the Preserved Tablets in heaven, and given to Mohammed by the angel Gabriel. Yet, there is a clear difference between the teaching of the Koran when Mohammed was in Mecca, at the beginning of his mission, and when he moved to Medina, at the end of his life.

While many of the verses from the Mecca period of his life were relatively peaceful in nature, they were replaced, or abrogated, by the violent verses of the Medina period. For instance, in the Mecca period, Mohammed said about those who refused his religion, "You have your religion, and I have mine."

This verse implies peaceful co-existence with Jews, Christians and even the pagans who populated the Arabian deserts.

But, after his military successes in Medina, Mohammed's tone changed. He no longer encouraged co-existence. Instead of accommodating the non-Muslims in the cities he conquered, he simply replaced abrogated the peaceful verses with ones encouraging violence against non-Muslims.

As I previously mentioned, this doctrine of abrogation was contrived to deal with the glaring inconsistencies between the Mecca and Medina chapters of the Koran.

Mohammed said, "Whatever communications we abrogate, or cause to be forgotten, we bring one better than it or like it. Do you not know that Allah has power over all things?"

In few places in the Koran is this doctrine of abrogation seen with such clarity as the issue of co-existence between Muslims and non-Muslims. In place of the aforementioned, peaceful verse, "You have your religion and I have mine," Mohammed brought the so-called "Verse of the Sword."

In soura 9:5, "When the sacred months are over, slay the idolaters wherever you find them. Arrest them, besiege them, and lie in ambush everywhere for them. If they repent and take to prayer and render the alms levy, allow them to go their way. God is forgiving and merciful."

This is one of the main verses used to incite against the supposed infidels and non- Muslims; there are many others.

In Soura 8:12 (Al Anfal), the Koran says, "I will cast terror into the hearts of those who disbelieve. Therefore strike off their heads, and strike off every fingertip of them."

There are over 160 such violent verses in the Koran. In addition to these verses that encourage violence, the whole subject of abrogation is completely inconsistent with what Mohammed taught about the Preserved Tablets in heaven. Islam teaches that Gabriel gave Mohammed the words from the immutable Preserved Tablets in heaven. How then could a verse that was the unchallenged word of God later be replaced by something better? Does God's word change? Does God change his mind? Were the Preserved Tablets also changed to be in line with the Koran that Gabriel brought to Mohammed?

This is a huge, glaring inconsistency in the whole doctrine of the Koran's perfection. According to many respected Muslim scholars, as many as 260 of the Koran's verses were "abrogated."

But while the peaceful verses were abrogated, when it comes to the presentation of Islam in the West, Muslims often focus on these "peaceful verses" to show that Islam encourages co-existence.

And while the media focus is on "peaceful jihad," or self-discipline, the Koran makes no such distinctions. The focus is military conquest, and the goal is uniting the world governments into an Islamic Caliphate.

The liberal media in the West has fallen for the "peaceful Islam" campaign that has swept the country. Although in the West, Islam presents the "Meccan" face of peace, the truth is that the "Meccan" verses have been abrogated, and the true Islam is reflected in the "Medina" verses that encourage violence and subjugation of non-Muslims. All one needs to do is look at the treatment of Christians and Christianity in Muslim countries to see that the whole "religion of peace" idea is a false one. In saying this, it must be pointed out, again, that the vast majority of Muslims are peaceful and have no desire for a violent overthrow of the government or social system in the West. But the problem is not Muslims; it is the undefiled, pure Islamic way of thinking.

I've heard it said that all faiths have those pesky, unfriendly and hateful verses. We see these "sprinkled in the Old Testament with Abraham, Moses, Caleb, David and others," as some have said. This is a statement some non-Christian theologians and apologists use as support in saying that all belief systems, including Christianity, have their shortfalls. Whether this be true or not, I would definitely have to say that if a belief system is formed well in the beginning, and then later seems to implode on itself with contradictions, one must take a step back and examine the teaching very carefully. It must be treated as a court case is treated. In a court there are witnesses, evidences, a jury and a judge. I often say that history is the judge, and the textual source is the evidence. The witness in this scenario would be our morality. Some may look at the evidence, and turn a blind eye, ignoring good conscious.

Now, one thing that we can all agree with is that God delivered the Ten Commandments to Moses within the dimension of time. First came the first commandment, then the second, then the third and so forth. It became something holy. Upon completion, the Law was birthed, and until this day, we have that Law, and it has affected society everywhere. The difference, however, between all these pesky, hateful verses is that within the context of Islamic history, and within time, the peaceful and loving verses of the Koran morphed into the "Medina" verses, evolving negatively from something beautiful into something very unattractive. Knowing that God works within the dimension of time, those Biblical verses, which are so often claimed to be hateful, became something quite the opposite. The old tribal ways of the Old Testament soon ended, and a better way came with the long awaited Messiah. The old ways became new ways, and a law fueled by love was enacted where enemies become friends, and hate is not allowed to exist. This is the difference between those verses.

These issues we have discussed are only a few of the many errors and inconsistencies in the Koran, but all of them combined are not the reason why I left Islam . . . which leads me to my next point.

CHAPTER 11

Why I am a Christian

The character and teachings of Mohammed combined with the errors and inconsistencies in the Koran did have an impact on me, but they are not the main reasons that I am not a Muslim.

Although these factors all united to help push me away from Islam, there had to have been an even more powerful force pulling me towards Christ. This power, I believe, was irresistible.

Looking back on my years as a Christian, I see there has been much heart ache and many troublesome times; there were many days of confusion and much loss. But there have also been many prayers answered. There have been many healings in Jesus' name. I have seen inexplicable signs that left me in awe. But, at the end of the day, there is one thing that drew me to Jesus Christ and has kept me all these years: LOVE.

At every moment of my life, at every crucial crossroad I stood at, wondering which way to go, there was one thing that I found so compelling: the love of Christ. The love of Jesus is an oasis in the deserts of our lives. It is a place where the weary man can go to receive the deep touch his heart longs for.

The love of Christ is not something we can fully understand, nor is it something we can fully grasp with our intellects. We can only truly know it by an encounter and a revelation.

I once was foolish. I thought that a man can be revived by seeing supernatural things. I was foolish to think that a mere miracle would win my people, and deliver them from the darkness of Islam.

Of course healings and miracles are a legitimate and valid way to win souls, but I have come to recognize that the lame man, who walked, all too soon, forgot the feeling of numbness in his legs. The man once wounded, all too soon, forgot the feeling of pain. The woman once acting in sinful ways, all too soon, forgot the deviance of her old ways.

All these were touched by God, but at the core of that touch, was the life-giving force of Christ's love. Although these may often forget the supernatural works of God in their lives, it is impossible for the unloved soul to forget the power of love which he has tasted.

Having experienced the darkness of rejection, it is impossible for one to forget that touch of Jesus Christ that assures him that he is, and will always be, loved.

I, myself, have received the wonderful nuggets of revelation hidden within the pages of the Bible. I have seen miracles performed in the name of Jesus. I have seen the providential hand of God so many times. But what gives me peace, at the end of this day, is not remembering these by-products of faith, rather it is the same thing that touched me back there in Jerusalem - love. It is simply knowing that I, who was rejected, have now found love that is pure. I found the agape kind of love, God's unconditional pure love. I have also found that unconditional love is the most effective way to bring about change in any life.

It's easy to resist someone who you fear might have hidden motives, but it is so hard to resist Jesus, the One Who loved us so much and gave all He was to show us that love. All He wants is to walk with us.

When He walked on the streets of Jerusalem, He allowed God's love to flow through Him to touch the multitudes, and God's love hasn't changed. God is still reaching people in that same way all over the world. "Now abides faith, hope and love, these three; but the greatest of these is love."

Jesus preached different messages to different people. Some listened to His words, and some ignored Him.

Muslims say he was a prophet. Jews say he was a psycho, and yet we Christians call him Lord.

He came with a message of peace, where others came with acts of war. He told Peter to put away his sword because He is the Prince of Peace and not war. His message was to be spread through acts of love and compassion.

He changed the lives of murderers and thieves with love. He forgave the adulteress. He forgave them all. Instead of shedding the blood of others, he allowed others to shed his blood. He never took the life of another. Instead, He gave away his own life.

He taught a better, higher law. He taught the law of life in the Holy Spirit, which is summed up in two commands: to love God with all our hearts, souls and strength, and to love our neighbors as ourselves.

He wasn't interested in politics, fame or fortune, and, yet, the politicians came to him. The famous knew him, and the wealthy gave away their possessions to follow him.

For disciples, He chose the uncultured. The sophisticated, He intimidated with His uncompromising holiness and love. Some people were told that He is just a man, but found out later that He was much more.

The moment you get serious with yourself, and with Him, your eyes will see His brilliant light, and you'll hear the words, "Call upon Me, and you shall be saved."

Napoleon had his few years of fame. Alexander the Great expanded his kingdom across the known world. Hitler claimed to be the great fuehrer, and brought most of Europe under his control. Mussolini was a ruthless dictator, and Stalin – an indescribable murderous tyrant.

But no other man in history ever dared to make such claims that Jesus made, "I am the resurrection and the life. He who believes in Me shall never die."

His love is unconditional. It has no barriers, no limits. His love quite often oversteps OUR insecurities. We may lock the door to our heart, and build huge walls around it, but He has the keys, and His love can walk through walls.

If you are small, He is big. If you are humble, he will exalt you. If you are proud, He will humble you. If you mourn, He will comfort you. If you're merciful, He'll give you mercy. For His yoke is easy. His burden is light.

As the Psalmist said, "The Lord is my light and my salvation, of whom shall I be afraid?? Billions of people through the ages, and across the world, have discovered these words to be true.

So what is salvation? It is deliverance from sin and its consequences brought out by faith in Christ.

Jesus looked at the Pilate, the man who could decide his fate, and fearlessly said that He was indeed a King.

Now you tell me. Was he just a prophet? Was He really a psycho? Doesn't

He sound like the King of kings and the Lord of lords?

There's a reason Jesus could look the governor in his face and challenge him, knowing His death was imminent. He knew the Father's love, and He knew there was no greater power in the universe.

It's the same reason why the disciples and early Christians could look at death in the face and choose martyrdom. They knew the Father. They knew the Son.

As John, the Beloved, would say, "That which our eyes have seen and our hands have handled."

As Peter would say, "We were eyewitnesses of His glory."

They saw Him when He was crucified and then they saw Him when He rose again. They knew He is the Truth. They simply couldn't deny it.

Many have died for what they believed to be true, but NO ONE has ever died for what they KNEW to be a LIE. Of those who followed him the closest, the 11 disciples, all but one, would die convinced of what they had seen and heard.

He is able to keep you from falling, and He is able to present you before God without fault, and with great joy.

For years, I allowed culture and tradition to tell me who Jesus was. One day, I decided to do something out of the ordinary in order to find out who Jesus truly was. I simply asked Him to show me. His reply to me was the encounter I received. This is the power of love. This is the power of Christ. He is love.

The aged Simeon held within his hands the baby Jesus while standing in the temple. He knew something that the others didn't. Luke tells us that Simeon blessed God and said, "Lord, now you are letting your servant die in peace, according to your word, for my eyes have seen your salvation."

The main objective for this aged man of God was to encounter his Messiah. He lived for this one moment. How bad did Simeon want to see the fulfillment of God's purpose for his life? How long did this old man wait for this one moment? After seeing Jesus, he deliberately embraced the end of his own life. He could now die in peace, for he saw the long awaited Messiah.

Luke also tells of Anna, a prophetess, who did not depart from the temple, but was constantly worshiping God with fasting and prayer. Upon seeing the baby Jesus, she began to give thanks to God, and to speak of the Christ child to all who were waiting for the redemption of Jerusalem.

These knew he was the Messiah. Did they know that He was the Son of God? Did they know He was God Incarnate?

In Mathew 16, Jesus asked Peter one of the most important questions ever asked of a man, "Who do men say that I am?"

No doubt, Peter answered sincerely, "Well some say that You're one of the prophets!"

But, as Jesus so often did with His disciples, He zeroes in on Peter, and asked a more probing question, "Who do YOU say that I am?"

And for the first time in history a man answered correctly.

Some had already acknowledged Him to be the Messiah, but Peter knew what that actually meant! I can imagine how, at that moment, time stood still, and all of heaven bowed the ear to Peter, waiting for the Lord to be recognized. It was at this moment when prophecy would be colliding with destiny, and both would be colliding with human history.

Peter said "You are the Christ, the Son of the living God."

To Jews and Muslims, one of the biggest stumbling stones is the divine Sonship of Jesus. It is, by far, the hardest thing for them to accept.

This is also one of the biggest areas of disagreement between Muslims and Christians. It's simply easier to accept the humanity of their prophets, rather than to accept that Jesus is both divine and human.

We must keep in mind that when Peter spoke those words, "You are the Christ, the Son of the Living God," even he didn't realize the enormity of what he was saying.

Jesus' response shows us how important Peter's words really were, "Blessed are you, Simon Bar-Jonah, for flesh and blood has not revealed this to you, but My Father who is in heaven. And I also say to you, that you are Peter, and on this rock, I will build My church, and the gates of Hades shall not prevail against it."

I'd like to be like Peter. It gives me hope to see how God could use someone like him. Just the way He can use someone like me. In Peter, we can see what God can do when a man gets a revelation of Jesus.

Allow me to explain this very intriguing relationship between Jesus and the man who knew Him first, Peter. One of the first stories we have about Peter is in the Gospel of John. Andrew told his brother Peter, "We have found the Messiah." And he brought him to Jesus.

Now when Jesus looked at him, He said, "You are Simon, the son of John, but you shall be called Peter (Petros in the Greek which is translated, a small stone).

In Middle Eastern cultures, a name is often a window into someone's personality. It can reveal clues about your destiny as well. We can see this repeatedly in the Old Testament where the name of Abram was changed to Abraham; Sarai to Sarah; and Jacob to Israel.

When Jesus and Simon meet for the first time, Jesus changes Simon's name to Peter. Why would he change it to Peter, which meant a small rock? What must have been going through Simon's mind at that point?

Did he think that by calling him "Peter," Jesus implied that he was rough around the edges, an unyielding and stubborn soul? Was Peter shaken because he knew that he really was hard-headed, hot-tempered, and emotionally-driven?

Three years later, Jesus would ask him, "Who do YOU say I am?"

Peter affirms the Christ, the Son of the Living God.

Jesus, at that moment, affirmed Peter, "Blessed are you Petros (small rock), for upon this Petra (immovable rock), I will build my church, and the gates of Hell will not prevail against it. For flesh and blood has not revealed this to you but my Father in heaven!"

At that moment, no doubt, it clicked in Peter's mind that the name change which occurred at his first meeting with Jesus, was not an insult. Rather it was a decree, a prophetic call for Peter to be what he would surely become, a world changer.

Basically, what Jesus was saying to Peter is, "I chose you, Peter, in spite of the fact that you are rough around the edges. Even though you're flakey, and easily moved by people's words and actions, I will use you. Even though you're hard-headed, hot tempered, emotionally driven, and even out of control at times, I am going to connect you to the Petra, the unshakeable mountain, and you won't always be swayed back and forth. When I get through with you, Peter, you will be dangerous to the enemy, and I will focus all your passion for a greater purpose!"

Andrew said how he had found the Messiah, but Peter went a step further in proclaiming that the Messiah is also the Son of the Living God.

This doesn't mean Peter was perfect. It just means he learned how to let Jesus be strong in those areas of his own weakness. This Gospel of Christ has empowered us who dare to believe.

Living downtrodden, and always defeated, is not the will of God. Often times, we wish to disqualify ourselves from the responsibility of actually doing something, as did Peter after his failure.

It can be intimidating to look at the darkness in the world, and to be told to turn on the lights! It's hard to look at the nations, and hear the cry of Jesus' heart urging us, "Go!"

It's just easier to be disqualified, but Christ's love compels us, and we are all without excuse.

Fast-forward in time a short while, add some trials, and pour in some tribulation, and what do you get?

Peter's Epic Failure

He denied Jesus three times, but what did Jesus do? He offered Peter hope. Christ intercepts Peter, while he was fishing. This tells us that Peter had put up his Apostle's mantle, and reverted to the family biz of fishing. Let's read that text from John 21.

Jesus said to Simon Peter, "Simon, son of Jonah, do you love Me more than these?"

Peter said to Him, "Yes, Lord, You know that I love You."

Jesus said to him, "Feed My lambs."

Jesus asked him again, a second time, "Simon, son of Jonah, do you love Me?"

Peter said to Him, "Yes, Lord, You know that I love You."

Jesus said to him, "Tend My sheep."

Jesus said to him the third time, "Simon, son of Jonah, do you love Me?"

Peter was grieved because He said to him the third time, "Do you love Me?"

And he said to Him, "Lord, You know all things; You know that I love You."

Why did Jesus ask him three times? This is a little hard to understand in the English because we only have one word for "love." The Greek language, on the other hand, has different words for love.

When Jesus first asked Peter, "Do you love me?," He was saying, "Peter, do you AGAPE Me?"

The response from the defeated disciple was "Lord, you know I PHILEO You."

Phileo means the emotional, brotherly love. But Jesus was asking about the unconditional, God-love implied by agape.

Agape is the God kind of love. It's the committed love which says, "Hurt me, kill me, curse me, and backstab me, YET I WILL STILL LOVE YOU." Agape is the complete, unbiased, unconditional, unselfish, unbreakable, unfailing type of love.

Phileo is the brotherly kind of love. It's human-to-human affection. Brothers love brothers, friends love friends.

In Greek there is also the eros kind of love. This is the sexual, romantic love between a man and his wife.

So Jesus asked, "Peter do you AGAPE me?"

Peter responded, "Lord, You know I PHILEO You."

Jesus was really asking, "Peter are you fully committed to me? Are you still in love with me despite the hurts and disappointments? Peter, are you REALLY devoted to me? Do you choose to love me and follow me, even in the hard times, when all hell breaks loose and everything within you wants to runaway and seek easy comfort!?"

Peter's response was, "Lord, You know I have brotherly love for you. I've got your back, sometimes. My love for you is very human in nature. I love you, Jesus, but with an incomplete commitment. It's human, it's not perfect, and this is where I'm at, Jesus!"

Jesus response here is incredible and SO EMPOWERING. Despite Peter's obvious lack of commitment, He says again, "Feed my sheep."

What was going through Peter's mind at this moment? What a moment it must have been when Jesus again asks if Peter loved him.

Peter answered as before.

Jesus said the same thing again, "Feed my sheep!"

And finally, Jesus asks again, but this time, with a twist. He asks "Peter, do you even PHILEO me?" Are you even that committed to Me? As you say? He put his finger on the depths of Peter's heart.

It's at this point that Peter was grieved in his heart, and said, "Lord, You know my heart; You know that I PHILEO You."

And a third affirmation of empowerment came from Jesus, "Then feed my sheep."

Peter's heart was grieved. Why was he grieved? He was sad because he, no doubt, WANTED to be completely given to Jesus. So Jesus offers him hope, and reinstates him as the Peter who got the awesome revelation in Matthew 16. And Jesus wanted him to be that as well. And Jesus, through His loving affirmations and probing of Peter's heart, reinstated him.

Why?

Verse 18 explains. Jesus tells him, "When you were young, you could do whatever you wanted, go wherever you wanted to go, but when you are old (when you are fully mature), Peter, you will stretch out your hands and go where you aren't able to go now (because of your lack of dedication). Jesus said this to hint at the kind of death, by which, Peter would glorify God.

Peter was now empowered so that one day, maybe not yet, but soon, Christ would perfect in him, love, and one day, He would be at the place of complete surrender to Jesus because Jesus never fails, and His faithfulness reaches above all unfaithfulness. That good work which began in you, my friend, like Peter, shall, and will, be complete. Jesus said so!

Chapter 12

The Final Step

Of the writing of books, there is no end, like Solomon said in the Book of Ecclesiastes. As I pondered the many steps I've taken in my life so far, I considered diligently why I should take this one, the writing of this book; the telling of my story.

I could write a long list of reasons why I should, or why I shouldn't, have written this book. I believe, first of all, that God wanted me to tell this story, my story. My story is by no means over. There are many steps ahead of me that are of greater consequence than the ones I've already taken.

At the end of his Gospel, the Apostle John says that he could not, in the 15,240 words he used to teach us about Jesus, tell all that there was to tell. In fact, he said the world, itself, could not contain all the books that could be written about the Word, Jesus.

In a similar way, this book is, first and foremost, about Jesus. It is about Him coming to me and changing me. It is about the miracles He did. It's about the ways that He protected me. It's about the ways that He stood with me. And, most of all, it's about the way He loves me.

Sometimes God doesn't tell us why He wants us to do something. He just tells us to do, and sometimes, through obeying His command, we will find out the reason.

He told me to tell you my story.

He told me to tell you about the steps I had to take, and I think I understand at least part of the reason why: to help you to take the steps that He is asking of you.

You, the reader of this book, are the focus of all Heaven's attention. For the few years that each one of us is allowed to walk on this earth, all of God's resources and passion are focused on us. He uses all the means in His power to get our attention off this petty world and onto His infinity.

You are the reason for this book. It is a message to you, personally, about His love for, and His plan for you, and His longing and desire for you.

There are two groups of people who are holding this book and reading it.

Group One is made up of those who have never accepted Jesus Christ in their hearts. Within Group One may be atheists, nominal Christians, Buddhists, animists, secular humanists, Jews or maybe like I was, Muslims.

To you, I want to make a plea. I told you my story in the best words I could use because I want you to know Him, the One Who filled my empty heart, and gave meaning to my meaningless existence: Jesus Christ.

He is a Man, but He is much more than a Man. He is right where you are sitting or standing right now. In fact, He is standing at the door of your heart, and He is knocking. He wants to come into your heart, and He wants to give you life, real life.

Jesus said that we have no life in ourselves. He is not speaking about the soul life that we all have, and by which we experience this world, and each other. He is speaking about Spirit Life. We were created to have Spirit Life inside of us, but we were cut off from this Spirit Life because of our sinful nature and our many sins. This Spirit Life only comes by accepting Jesus Christ into our hearts.

This book has, so far, been about my steps. But in these closing pages, it will be about your step. There is a step that no one else, but you, my reader, can take. Even God, Who loves you with a love that cannot be fathomed or understood by our limited minds, cannot take this step for you.

Only you can.

Since I took this step, I want to urge you to do the same. Open the door of your heart. Let Jesus come in. He will satisfy your longing and empty heart. He will fill your empty life. I wouldn't be able to tell you these words unless I knew them to be true.

I experienced this life, this love myself. No one else can give you this life. No one else can give you this love. Your heart is crying out for this reconciliation with God, and I urge you to accept His free offer of salvation.

You may ask, "How do I open this door of my heart? How do I take this step?"

It is so simple. First of all, acknowledge that you have disobeyed God in your lifetime. The Bible says, "All have sinned and fallen short of the glory of God."

Secondly, ask God to forgive you for those sins, and repent. Turn away from those sins.

Thirdly, acknowledge that you need help. You don't need religion. You need a Savior. Jesus Christ is that Savior. He's the One who came and died on the cross for all those sins you committed and will ever commit.

Fourth, ask Jesus to come into your heart and be your Lord and Savior.

Fifth, pray this prayer. Say, "Dear God, I am a sinner. I have disobeyed You so many times. Please forgive me for all my sins. I want to turn away from my sins and follow you. Jesus, I believe that You are the Son of God who came to earth to save me. I believe You died on the cross, and rose again after three days, to save me. Thank You, Jesus, for dying for me. Come into my heart, and fill me with the Holy Spirit. I want to serve You every day for the rest of my life. Amen."

If you have prayed this prayer from your heart, and mean it, the Bible says that all your sins have been forgiven. Jesus shed His blood on the cross to give you forgiveness and new life. The Bible also says that you have become a member of God's family. God is now your father and you are His child.

There are four things that I would encourage you to do in order to grow in your relationship with God:

1. Pray every day.

This simply means to take some time every day to talk to God. He loves you and loves to hear your voice. He longs to spend time with you in this way.

2. Read the Bible.

The Bible is God's love letter to you. It shows you His will for your life, and how much He cares for you, and is willing to help you.

3. Get into a Bible-believing church and be committed to it.

It is so important that you be around other believers. Christians aren't perfect, and churches aren't perfect, but we are all learning and growing together. We need each other as the family of God.

4. Tell others about your faith in Jesus Christ.

Share Him, so they, too, can experience this love relationship with Him.

As well, I would love to hear from you. Please contact me at my web page: WWW.HAZEMFARRAJ.COM

Group Two are those of you who have already accepted Christ into your heart.

Like the first group, this group is made up of many categories: victorious Christians, stagnant Christians; backslidden Christians.

To those who would consider themselves in the "victorious" category, I hope this book inspired you to be all you can for the Lord, and to continue in your pursuit of greater holiness, intimacy and fruit for the Kingdom of God.

For those of you who consider yourselves stagnant, I hope this book will help inspire you to discover where in your walk that you became stagnant. When did you stop moving forward? When did you stop going deeper? When did you stop pursuing the Lord with all your heart?

Quite often, there was a choice made. There was something we didn't want to give up. There was something we didn't want to stop doing. There was a relationship we didn't want to break off. There was a relationship we didn't want to enter into. There was an offense that we didn't want to forgive.

I pray that you will make a choice today to find exactly when, and how, you stagnated, so that you can know where you can start again on your journey, to reach greater heights and greater depths in Him. His love is endless. His grace is boundless, and He is waiting to commence the journey with you.

The third, and perhaps the most difficult, category is that of the backslidden Christian. You may have reached this point in the book, and still be in a desperately empty condition. You may be attending church, and may even be a minister of the Gospel, and, still, you find yourself in a desperate backslidden condition.

As with the stagnant Christian, the backslidden Christian made a choice, at some point, to leave off the way of wisdom, and to pursue the path of pleasures, or worldliness. Maybe you are a college student, and the secular humanism that you are faced with every day in school, has been chipping away at your faith. Maybe you have been successful in your pursuits, and have found acceptance with people who do not share your convictions and faith in Jesus Christ. Maybe you are trapped in some lustful addictions or drug addictions.

There are so many ways to drift away from our focus on Him. But He never drifts away from us. He is waiting for you to return home. Please don't just disregard these warnings. None of us knows how many more times God will call us to repent and return. The days are evil, and the tendency to drift gets stronger, as the pull and lure of the world increases in sinfulness and hardness.

Please take to heart the words of Jesus, "Remember from where you have fallen. Go back and do the first works."

Come back to Jesus today. The world is an empty place that will, in the end, lead us astray. Stop running from Him. The pleasures of the world are temporary, and they end up costing us our very lives. Sin will take you farther than you ever thought you'd stray. Sin will keep you longer than you ever thought you'd stay. Sin will cost you more than you ever thought you'd pay.

Here's a recommended prayer. Say, "Heavenly Father, forgive me for time away from You. Father, I want to stop running away from You and Your will. I want to follow You. This world is so deceiving, and yet I have fallen so much, that, at times, I wonder if I could ever find my way back. Help me, Father, to come back to You. Help me to let go of the things that bind me. Create, in me, a clean heart. Renew a right spirit in me. Make me willing to do Your will. In Jesus' Name."

I pray that this book has been a blessing and inspiration to you. I pray that God will use it to inspire you to be all you can be for Him, and to use the time you have on earth to serve Him, and to bring Him glory, and to bring many people to Him. In the awesome name of Jesus.

Amen.

Special Moments

Pictured with the Bajalia Family and my "lil bro" Jarad. These are those who selflessly came across the globe to tell me about Jesus. Isa, Alene and Jarad: You guys are major blessings to me and thank you for loving me good.

I am welcoming Arthur Blessitt to discuss his walk around the world. Arthur Blessitt is one of the most humble men I have ever met in my life. Without exaggeration, this man is the real deal. His story is mind blowing.

I had the opportunity to speak with Benny Hinn on Reflections. He talked about the trials and hardships of growing up in an Arabic Middle Eastern family. This was a highlight for me since God broke the depression as I was watching his program. Isn't it interesting how life brings us back full circle.

Snapshot from TBN as Dr Crouch had a word of wisdom for me. I have learned to listen to this man. He is a pioneer and an amazing blessing to the propagation of the Gospel in our times. I love him very much for how he has poured into me and allowed me to be a part of his life.

Matthew Barnett was our honored guest on this episode of Reflections. We were on the top floor of the amazing Dream Center in LA. Matthew Barnett is a tremendous answer to prayer for so many people.

The Holy City. My heart burns for Jerusalem and I am trusting the Lord that soon and very soon He shall reign from this Holy Hill.

This is the Church where I witnessed Steve and the other believers worshipping. This is the place where that took place in Jerusalem.

Enjoying laughs with friends on Reflections.

The Saylor Family: People who loved me well and took me into their home to share with me what a beautiful healthy family looks like. I love them very much and words will never suffice the things which should be spoken about Pastor Harry Saylor and his family.

Pictured with Fox News TV Personality, Glenn Beck.

At Dr Crouch's 77th Birthday Celebration. We had fun that evening celebrating his life and our friendship with other close friends.

I am seated at the empty tomb of Jesus Christ. The plaque on the door says "He is not here, He is risen." I thought it was befitting our Savior.

Elsa Brown. She has been there for me through thick and thin. Even when she had every right to give up on me, she stayed beside me and never gave up. It is one of my prized relationships that I honor with my life.

With Vice President Dan Quayle.

This is me in the midst of my 12th grade school year. Little did I know that shortly after this picture was taken, my life and destiny would take a dramatic turn. You can see that the depression had been taking its toll on me. I was gaining weight even then. I was 17 years old here in 2002.

This is on the Palestinian side of the dreaded separation wall which many Palestinians in Bethlehem stare at every day. They literally use artwork and graffiti to express themselves. I stood here because I thought this was the only thing that changes lives. Pure - Simple - Love.

Pictured with Steve Mashni my elder brother and friend in the faith. I am forever grateful to you Steve.

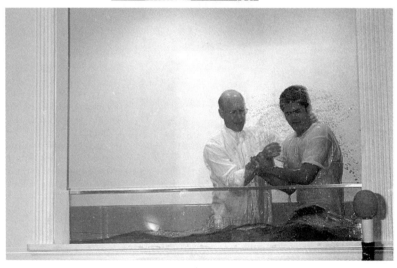

www.hazemfarraj.com

www.Facebook.com/HazemFarraj
www.Facebook.com/ReflectionsTv

https://twitter.com/hazem_f

www.Youtub eflectionsTV

If you would like to learn more about Hazem Farraj, or to have him share at your congregation or event, please contact us at the information provided. Hazem would be honored to hear from you. He believes God has called him to share a life-giving message to the world, and will be most glad to come communicate to you and yours.

Website: www.hazemfarraj.com
E-mail: Reflectionstv@live.com